Skills *in*
EXISTENTIAL
Counselling & Psychotherapy

Series Editor
Francesca Inskipp

Skills in Counselling & Psychotherapy is a series of practical guides for trainees and practitioners. Each book takes one of the main approaches to therapeutic work and describes the core skills and techniques used within that approach.

Topics covered include

♦ how to establish and develop the therapeutic relationship
♦ how to help the client change
♦ how to assess the suitability of the approach for the client.

This is the first series of books to look at skills specific to the different theoretical approaches, making it ideal for use on a range of courses which prepare the trainees to work directly with clients.

Books in the series:

Skills in Transactional Analysis Counselling & Psychotherapy
Christine Lister-Ford

Skills in Person-Centred Counselling & Psychotherapy
Janet Tolan

Skills in Cognitive-Behavioural Counselling & Psychotherapy
Frank Wills

Skills in Rational Emotive Behaviour Counselling & Psychotherapy
Windy Dryden

Skills in Gestalt Counselling & Psychotherapy, Second Edition
Phil Joyce & Charlotte Sills

Skills *in*
EXISTENTIAL
Counselling & Psychotherapy

Emmy van Deurzen
and Martin Adams

Los Angeles | London | New Delhi
Singapore | Washington DC

First published in 2011

SAGE Publications Ltd
1 Oliver's Yard
55 City Road
London EC1Y 1SP

SAGE Publications Inc.
2455 Teller Road
Thousand Oaks, California 91320

SAGE Publications India Pvt Ltd
B 1/I 1 Mohan Cooperative Industrial Area
Mathura Road
New Delhi 110 044

SAGE Publications Asia-Pacific Pte Ltd
3 Church Street
#10-04 Samsung Hub
Singapore 049483

Library of Congress Control Number: 2009941993

British Library Cataloguing in Publication data

A catalogue record for this book is available from the British Library

ISBN 978-1-4129-4779-4
ISBN (pbk) 978-1-4129-4780-0

Typeset by C&M Digitals (P) Ltd, Chennai, India
Printed and bound by CPI Group (UK) Ltd, Croydon, CR0 4YY
Printed on paper from sustainable resources

To Penny and Digby

'The unexamined life is not worth living'
Socrates

CONTENTS

Acknowledgements   x
About the Authors   xi

Introduction   1

1   The Framework of Existential Therapy   **7**

Theoretical background and history   7
Some of the major existential philosophers   13
Limits of human living: the givens of existence   15
Living in time   22
Living with paradox   23
Anxiety and the givens of existence   24
The mind and the body   24

2   The Person of the Therapist   **27**

Who are you?   27
The use of life experience to reflect on life and its meanings   27
Being–with: reciprocity and trust collaboration   30
Capacity for self-reliance and individuality   33
Transparency and wisdom   34
Who are you as a therapist?   35
The importance of personal therapy in your training   36
How to use supervision?   37

3   Working Phenomenologically: The Centre of Existential Therapy   **39**

Phenomenology: assumptions, biases, blind spots and the worldview   39
The assumptions of existential therapy   41
Questioning assumptions   41
Working phenomenologically   42

4   Developing an Existential Attitude   **57**

Openness to experience   57
Boundaries and consistency   60

Mutuality and dialogue   63
Self-disclosure   65
Directiveness, directness and direction   69

5 From Theory into Practice   71

Expression and self-expression: the paradox of the self   71
Identifying themes and issues   73
Identifying values and beliefs   76
Emotions as a compass   80
Choice and responsibility   89
Anxiety: authenticity, guilt and bad faith   91
Working with dreams and the imagination   96

6 What Really Matters to the Client   101

Some first principles   101
Dilemmas, conflicts and tensions   102
The physical dimension. Coming face to face with life and death:
    the reality of change and loss, in the *Umwelt*.   105
The social dimension. Isolation and connectedness: relationships in the *Mitwelt* 107
The personal dimension. Freedom and a personal sense of integrity:
    life patterns and the original project in the *Eigenwelt*   113
The spiritual dimension. Consistency of values, beliefs and
    principles in the *Überwelt*   117

7 The Process of Existential Therapy   123

Existential therapy as storytelling   123
Meeting, assessment and diagnosis   124
Note taking   126
The influence of the frame and the context of therapy   126
The first session and the contract   128
Length of the contract   130
Fees   131
The beginning and end of sessions   132
Working through, reluctance and resistance   133
Endings and termination   135
Therapy as a learning process   137

8 Putting it All Together: Summing Up   144

Summarizing the philosophical basis of existential practice   144
Summarizing the principles of existential practice   145
Developing a personal style   149

••• Contents •••

Glossary	150
Bibliography	156
Index	160

ACKNOWLEDGEMENTS

We would like to acknowledge the debt we owe to past teachers and colleagues who have encouraged us to persist with our existential explorations over the years. In a different way we are indebted to all those we have differed with – for they have helped us to refine and clarify our ideas in ways that would otherwise not have been possible.

We would particularly like to thank all the students and trainees at the New School of Psychotherapy and Counselling: you are the ones who have required us to explain and clarify the practicalities of existential therapy in ever more precise and accurate ways, for you have always asked the best questions.

Finally we each want to acknowledge the love and support of our spouses, Digby and Penny, without which this book would simply not have been written.

ABOUT THE AUTHORS

Emmy van Deurzen is a world authority on the existential approach. She has founded both the School at Regent's College and the New School of Psychotherapy and Counselling and directs NSPC as well as her private practice, Dilemma Consultancy.

Martin Adams is a practitioner and supervisor in private practice and a Lecturer at the New School of Psychotherapy and Regents College, both in London. He is also a sculptor.

INTRODUCTION

This is the very perfection of a man, to find out his own imperfections.

Saint Augustine

Existential therapy has a long-established tradition of over a century of theory and practice and all existential therapists have two things in common: they base their work primarily on philosophy rather than on psychology, and are fundamentally suspicious of technique and skills-based practice. They believe that human problems need to be tackled by thinking about them in the broadest possible terms with the aim of clarifying and elucidating them as part of the difficulties and dilemmas of the human condition. This means that existential therapists, unlike other therapists, are more concerned about doing justice to the way clients live their lives, rather than to eradicate specific problems or focus on particular symptoms of discomfort and unease. The aim is to help people get better at facing up to difficulties with courage instead of running away from them. This means that existential therapists have traditionally steered clear of formulating their approach in terms of the acquisition of skills or the application of particular techniques. They have always argued that technique and skills get in the way of a full understanding of what a person is truly preoccupied with. They have taken the view that theories and methods of counselling and therapy can distort the way in which we consider what it means to be human. Existential therapists aim to go beyond the various perspectives on psychotherapy and counselling in order to achieve a truly philosophical view of each person's predicament. This means that existential work has always remained a very private and to some extent obscure and even arcane form of therapy. It is outside of the mainstream partly because existential therapists have refused to pin down their ways of working. They value their freedom of practice and have never formulated the steps of existential therapy in a systematically principled way. This has often meant that existential therapists have borrowed techniques from other methods and have integrated these into their work when they were compatible with an overall philosophical approach. This integration is done in a disciplined way. It is most definitely not an 'anything goes' model. Existential therapists are ready to engage with other therapeutic methods when appropriate, but do so in a philosophical and therefore critically aware manner. They seek to test, debate and research the assumptions made by theories in practice. Philosophy, as a search for truth and love of wisdom, is committed to such questioning, and existential therapy is no exception.

There has been a long-standing tension between existential and psychoanalytic ways of working, from the early correspondence and lifelong friendship between

Freud and Binswanger onwards. Existential authors have long questioned the theoretical foundation of psychoanalysis, disagreeing primarily with its biological and often reductionist worldview and paternalistic power base. Existential therapists are equally cautious about cognitive behavioural therapies and their haste in identifying and fixing problems before these have been fully understood. They have also had a problematic relationship with humanistic and person-centred approaches although the origins and epistemology of these methods owe much to the existential tradition. The positivistic assumptions about human nature that most humanistic practitioners (and positive psychologists) hold, are not compatible with a rigorous philosophical approach. The existential tradition has probably most in common with the movement of disciplined psychotherapy integration, where such integration is based on well-thought-through principles and research. It also has many points of contact with systemic approaches when these are based on understanding individual experience within a context.

Existential therapy is a form of therapy that frequently appeals to those who have been in the therapeutic field for some time and whose personal experience has made them question therapeutic dogma. It appeals most when what we want is a practical theory or a principled practice that truly relates to people's concrete preoccupations and aims in life. Existential therapy is especially appreciated by people who contend with the pressures and contradictions of cross-cultural work, because it provides a relatively value-free basis from which to work and does not prescribe a personality theory that is culturally limiting. For this reason it is relevant to internationally based work and more than normally compatible with spiritual practices that value individuals to be personally and socially responsible.

The existential tradition has evolved in different directions in different countries. In Continental Europe, it has tended towards a more structured and disciplined practice as, for instance, with Daseins analysis, which is a form of Heideggerian psychoanalysis, developed by Medard Boss in Switzerland. Or as Logotherapy, which was developed by Victor Frankl in Austria. In the United States, existential therapy has tended to be associated with the Humanistic tradition and is then often known as Humanistic-Existential therapy or Humanistic-Integrative therapy. This is the case with the work of Kirk Schneider and Betty Cannon, who owe much to Person-centred therapy and Gestalt therapy respectively.

By virtue of our history and location, this book represents the British model of existential therapy, which is closer to its philosophical roots and based on the phenomenological method. In the British school also there are several tendencies and there is a division between two broad schools. On the one hand, there is what is often termed phenomenological-existential therapy, but which is actually a phenomenological variant of person-centred and/or integrative (Egan three-stage model-based) therapies (as with the work of Ernesto Spinelli, Dave Mearns and Mick Cooper). On the other hand, there is the radical existential approach of Emmy van Deurzen and her colleagues, which is firmly based on Continental philosophy. This book is broadly based on the latter.

Of course, the field of existential therapy is dynamic and in continuous transformation. Some cognitive therapists are already borrowing existential principles to enhance the practice of third wave CBT, and positive psychotherapists are similarly claiming to address existential issues. It is part of the existential tradition to keep philosophy's benefit wide open and let anyone who is interested take advantage of the clarity of its thinking without dictating how this should be done.

The breadth of the existential influence is very much related to its reluctance to pinpoint its own form of practice and to keep its therapeutic practice flexible enough to invite all comers and this should be seen as an advantage rather than as a disadvantage. It only becomes a problem if practitioners try to make it look as if they have the one and only claim to defining the existential approach. It is crucial to the future freedom of existential therapy that no one single form of existential therapy should be seen as the standard or definitive way of practising (Cooper, 2003; Deurzen and Arnold-Baker, 2005; Deurzen and Kenward, 2005; Deurzen and Young 2009).

This naturally makes it problematic to write a book on existential skills, which by definition is in contradiction with the existential enterprise of openness, suspension of certainty and technological over-simplification. There will be many existential therapists who will raise their eyebrows at the assumption that existential therapists actually do have a contribution to make to a literature of this nature, and these people will be reluctant to read this book. This is a shame because it will become obvious throughout the pages of this book that this contribution is not as tightly skills-based as that of other approaches. The skills of existential therapists are more of the ideological, critical or methodological kind than of the pragmatic and practical kind. For existential therapists it will never be possible to work strictly by the book – or even by *this* book. There are no absolute rules and regulations of existential therapy that can be prescribed and followed. It is rather a case of learning to work spontaneously and creatively and constantly go beyond previous knowledge as we extend ourselves to other human beings and learn more about the trials and tribulations of humankind. The relationship of theory to practice is crucial and it is one which we believe has not received enough coherent attention. It is likely that some of the things that you will come across in these pages will be familiar to you from other therapeutic perspectives. This is not a problem and just goes to show that some elements of other practices, but not all, can be consistent with existential practice.

To be true to existence, existential practice can neither be solely technical nor can it be entirely made up on the spot. This a paradox – it has to be both/and, not either/or. We hope in these pages we have described this paradox clearly enough for readers to understand how to work with them in the necessarily unpredictable environment of psychotherapy.

The skills of existential therapists are essentially derived from the qualities of human living and from the human capacity for formulating their own thinking about the world. This is always about drawing conclusions and learning from experience in a coherent and productive manner. Existential therapists are trained in philosophy and they learn to apply ideas and clear thinking to their practice. This is why existential therapists have a valuable contribution to make to supervision (Deurzen and Young, 2009) where this skill of taking an intellectual and philosophical overview of what is going on comes into its own. Similarly, existential therapy is particularly good in crisis situations and transitions, when people's worldviews come crashing down and they find it difficult to accept any other form of therapy, as they feel easily irked and offended by the certainty of therapeutic skills and views of human beings that are based on security and prescription.

Perhaps the most prominent skills of experienced existential therapists consist of being able to take the long view, to be tolerant, to be lenient and to have a robust philosophical sense of the overall tasks of human living, even when a person is in despair or when their life is coming apart at the seams. This is when existential therapy truly rises to the challenge. When the chips are down and all that needs to be done is for a person to lick their wounds, existential therapy can encompass the trauma, because of its global sense of human existence. People often find that they are able to gather great strength in this process and achieve a completely new understanding of life. Existential therapists are unlikely to be overawed by chronic or acute unhappiness. They do not expect people to live exemplary or constantly happy lives, and neither do they exact parental perfection. They work with what is real and actual and they accept imperfection, trouble, labour, pain and difficulty alongside the human need to perfect and ease their lives in order to build a new future.

The aim is always for people to become more clear, more aware and more able to understand themselves and the world of objects, other people and ideas and to extend and expand this understanding until it works optimally in practice. In this process, existential therapists use theory and thoughtfulness as tools towards elucidation. In the following pages we shall try to sharpen this theory and thoughtfulness in readers, without proposing a fixed package of skills that can simply be taught and applied although from time to time some specific interventions will be described. The reader is reminded that such skill practice should not to be taken too literally. It is important to take the spirit of the intervention and integrate it into your own way of working. The aim of the book is to help you live and work with an existential attitude. Nevertheless, it will be obvious that existential therapy is a specific craft, which it is possible to acquire and perfect and for which there are certain aptitudes and attitudes that help and others that hinder.

It is based on the human ability to reflect, and what emerges is that human beings have the capacity to draw new and special knowledge from their experience and thrive on their problems and the effort of overcoming them. Indeed, the human spirit soars most when it has to tackle difficulties and challenges. Although human beings have developed through biological evolution, reflection and consciousness have enabled us to go beyond a purely mechanical life. Human evolution is now most evident in the way we think about the world and in how we change ourselves to act on it more effectively. This comes at a cost – that of personal responsibility. There is no excuse for not clearly formulating this capacity for dialectical progress even though the practice of existential therapy will always remain a very personal business, much like an art form, interpreted differently by the different artists who are existential therapists. Even art has a technical basis, but it only becomes art when the techniques are owned and transcended. This we achieve by teaching ourselves new and sharper ways to observe and perceive reality and connect these with the brushstrokes that flow from knowing our medium. Similarly, it will become clear that to practise existential therapy we need to know our medium, which is that of human existence. We need to train ourselves to cultivate an attitude of open and engaged attentiveness, not just to the person in front of us, but to the life they lead, and the ways in which their particular problems can be resolved while at the same time resolving and throwing light on some general human issues that we all have in common. In order to hone this kind of attentiveness and intentionality, there are many aspects of practice we can train. This book will describe these and show how such ways of being can be honed and skilfully applied to therapy.

We shall start by looking at the overall framework of existential therapy in Chapter 1, specifying what a philosophical approach to therapy is about and how it replaces a psychological assessment with an assessment of the person's way of being in the world at many different levels. Then we shall go on to consider the person of the existential therapist in Chapter 2, looking at the specific ways of being that such therapists need to be capable of and the precise skills and aptitudes that they have to bring to the work with the client. Chapter 3 will describe the practice of phenomenology, that revolutionary observational and research method that underpins the existential approach and provides it with a systematic methodology to re-search the client's life style and their way of seeing the world. Chapter 4 will look at some of the basic principles of existential work and how to develop an existential attitude. It demonstrates with examples how such practice can be adopted. Then in Chapter 5 we will move on to linking theory and practice when we work with emotions and anxiety in particular. Chapter 6 will come back to the idea of worldview and define the preoccupations of the client as the beginning and end point of any therapeutic intervention, showing how existential therapists deal with the concrete problems that clients bring. In Chapter 7 we will see some elements of the process of existential therapy illustrated and worked with. In Chapter 8 we will summarize our findings and give a brief outline of the practice of existential therapy. Finally, you will find a glossary of terms that briefly clarifies some of the rather complex and complicated concepts any discussion of existential therapy contains. So while this book may not provide a simple outline list of skills that are useful to existential therapists, it will certainly pinpoint the aptitudes and intentions of therapists who are serious about practising this kind of therapy. This is a therapy that is firmly based on philosophy and that seeks to enable clients to think for themselves. It requires first and foremost that the therapist learns to live existentially. This means to think for yourself and to take responsibility for your thoughts, feelings and actions.

There are many other books on existential psychotherapy that can be used to supplement this introductory text (Yalom (1980), Deurzen (2002, 2010), Cohn (1997), Spinelli (2005, 2009), Strasser (1999)). But none of these texts have boldly formulated the skills of existential therapy, since these authors were all too aware that it would be foolish to try to summarize a practice that has to remain loosely defined if it is to continue doing justice to its own roots and objectives. Perhaps we are treading foolishly on territory where angels have not dared to tread before, but it seemed important in light of the current moves in psychotherapy provision and regulation, that the existential approach should speak up for itself and articulate its principles, methods, and skills. Having said this, we need to bear in mind that the existential approach will always try to go beyond these principles, methods, and skills. It will ultimately remain based on freedom.

This kind of book can only succeed if it is able to bring the various principles of practice to life for the reader and the vignettes and examples are designed to do this. There is always a confidentiality issue with this sort of material and all the examples we have used are fictional. But while they may not have historical truth, we believe they have narrative and existential truth. As Picasso said, 'We all know that Art is not truth. Art is a lie that makes us realize truth' (Fry, 1966: 165). This is another paradox, that fiction is a lie that helps us to see the truth. So all examples are derived directly from experience and yet entirely invented. If any of the examples ring a bell for any reader, then this is a measure of our success at being able to tell a lie that tells the truth.

To paraphrase the qualifying statement that appears in many novels and films – any similarity to any person alive or dead is simultaneously accidental, coincidental and deliberate.

1

THE FRAMEWORK OF EXISTENTIAL THERAPY

Change alone is eternal, perpetual, immortal

Schopenhauer

THEORETICAL BACKGROUND AND HISTORY

Introducing existential therapy

The questions that existential philosophers address are the questions that human beings have always asked themselves but for which they have never found satisfactory answers. This makes them both familiar and problematic. They are questions like:

- What does it mean to be alive?
- Why is there something rather than nothing?
- How should I act and be in relation to other people?
- How can I live a worthwhile life?
- What will happen after I die?

These are also the questions which clients are preoccupied with.

In spite of this familiarity there are some good reasons why existential ideas are not well known in psychotherapy. First, existential therapy does not have a single founding author with which it can be identified; it has no Freud, Rogers, Perls or Pavlov.

Second it has its roots in philosophy, which in spite of its intimate connections to the questions of living and its long history, has always been a rather academic discipline. All therapeutic perspectives have a philosophical basis but this is rarely acknowledged.

Because of their practical training, most therapists and counsellors are not used to exploring questions in a philosophical manner. They often focus on psychological and behavioural symptoms or on concrete aspects of professional interaction.

Although all existential thinkers have the philosophical stance in common, they can hold quite differing views and it is this dynamism and diversity that give the existential approach its particular strength and resilience. Nevertheless, it is the family resemblances that allow us to identify the characteristic skills and interventions of existential counselling and therapy that we will describe in these pages. We will be concentrating on how to explore our clients' human questions philosophically.

As we said in the Introduction, trying to delineate 'existential skills' is problematic because systematization and technique have generally been avoided in favour of personal freedom and responsibility. Existential therapists are reluctant to say: 'This is how you do existential therapy' because one of the central principles of existential therapy is that each therapist has to create his or her own personal way of working. But it is most definitely not a free-for-all. Existential therapy is an enquiry into meaning and any enquiry that is not systematic will lead to haphazard results and will be influenced by what the researcher wishes to find. Therefore it has characteristic structures, actions, disciplined interventions and specific skills to guide this enquiry and the task of existential therapists is to make these their own. They are based on the same broad structures that underpin phenomenological research. Indeed, existential philosophy is the result of the application of the phenomenological research method to the study of existence.

Before we go any further, a word of caution is necessary about some specialist words. Many everyday words like 'choice' and 'anxiety' are used in the existential tradition in a special sense, and this needs to be borne in mind. Conversely, there are many unfamiliar words like 'being-in-the-world' or 'thrownness' that sound daunting, but which actually refer to familiar experiences. These too will be explained.

What do we mean by 'philosophical'?

So what does it mean when we describe the existential approach to psychotherapy as philosophical? A wide range of philosophical writing is available to therapists, but not all philosophy is relevant, since it does not all deal with human or moral issues. Much of early Greek philosophy, Eastern philosophy and nineteenth- and twentieth-century Continental philosophy is relevant. Most of analytical philosophy is not so pertinent to therapy. Counsellors and therapists wishing to work in an existential manner do not necessarily need to have a thorough grounding in this literature and philosophical heritage. But they do have to develop some philosophical method in their thinking about life.

Other therapeutic approaches are primarily biological, psychological, social, intellectual or spiritual in nature and generally neglect philosophy. They also concentrate on what goes on inside an individual or between people and rarely extend to considering the human condition and its wider philosophical and socio-political context. Most therapies also focus on what is wrong and describe this as pathology and state that their objective is to cure a person of this. They are mostly concerned with intra-psychic or inter-personal factors. While existential therapy may also accommodate these dimensions at different times, its field of vision is wider and reaches beyond individual problems to life itself. Its focus is on the nature of truth and reality rather than on personality, illness or cure, so rather than thinking about function and dysfunction, it prefers to think in terms of a person's ability to meet the challenges that life inevitably presents us with.

Although the existential approach clearly involves ideas, it is not simply intellectual like a crossword puzzle and is certainly not abstract like mathematics. Understanding life is as crucial to survival as the ability to talk, walk, breathe or eat. It is practical and concrete. It is always life that is the teacher, and ideas are no use unless they can make a positive difference to our lives.

Action based on experience is everyone's first language. In this sense, existential therapy is the practical application of philosophy to everyday living. It is about coming to understand and therefore live productively and creatively within the constraints and possibilities of life. To engage with existential ideas requires us to have the courage to value diversity over uniformity, concreteness over abstractness, open-ended dilemmas over simplistic answers, and personally discovered and hard-earned authority over pre-existing dogmas and established power.

Fundamentally the skills of the existential therapist begin with the phrase inscribed at the Temple of Apollo at Delphi, 'Know thyself' because we cannot understand anyone or anything until we first understand ourselves and our relationship to human existence. This means that our primary tool as therapists is ourselves and our understanding of life, not theory or technique.

But even this is not so simple since we are always changing and we are also permanently and fundamentally in relationship with others. What this means is that one can never ignore the needs of others when making personal decisions but neither can one allow others to entirely determine oneself even when alone. This is a paradox.

What do we mean by 'existential'?

The German philosopher Martin Heidegger and the French philosopher Jean-Paul Sartre both agreed that existence comes before essence. What this means is that the fact *that* we are is more basic than *what* we are. We *are* first and define ourselves later. Moreover, we are always in a process of becoming something else. A person is first and foremost dynamic, alive, self-reflective and changing and this is the most important characteristic: *that* we exist, *that* we are alive and *that* we can transform ourselves, be aware and learn. For example, the essence of this book is that it is about the skills involved in existential therapy. But this book will always be this book; it will never change and also will not be able to change itself. A person is different at different times. We are dynamic, responsive and interactive. In one sense a person's essence is their chemical composition, e.g. as 85 per cent water. In another sense, a person is their genetic constitution, made up of half of each parent's gene pool. In yet another sense we can be said to be the result of our early experiences and education. Or we can say we are defined by the bio-chemical processes in our brains. Existentially, a person is clearly far more than any and all of this.

Let's consider the following incomplete sentence:

Fundamentally people are …

If we were to say that essence is more fundamental than existence, it could be completed in many different ways depending on one's view of human nature, for example:

Fundamentally, people are their DNA, or

Fundamentally, people are out for themselves, or

Fundamentally, people are social beings, or

Fundamentally, people are made in the likeness of a god.

The fact that we can talk about the human essence in so many different ways explains why there are so many different theories of psychotherapy, because they all consider essence to be prior to existence and they all have different views of what constitutes this essence.

But if it is true that existence precedes essence, the above sentence can only be completed with a full stop:

Fundamentally, people are.

That we exist and how we exist determine the essence that emerges, not the other way round. This is the first principle that all existential philosophers share: that their primary concern is the existence of human beings. It is also the most significant defining characteristic of existential therapy. A therapeutic approach can be described as existential if it accepts this premise.

This is of course not the end of the matter by any means. If people are primarily without a fixed essence, then their life becomes a matter of personal interpretation, responsibility and choice. What we take as being our essence, our nature, our sense of self, in fact evolve over time and are a consequence of the way we interpret the fundamental givens, the boundaries, of existence. We only see it as fixed because it evokes too much anxiety, existential anxiety, to acknowledge its innate flexibility and fluidity.

It is the capacity for thinking and reflecting on the constraints of our existence that creates a sense of self and it is this reflection that plays the major role in what we are. It is our understanding that allows us to choose whether we let ourselves be defined by circumstance or find a way to meet life's challenges.

EXERCISE

Make a list of six different identities, characteristics or talents you think you have. For example:

- parent
- son/daughter
- gardener
- therapist
- bi-lingual
- student

Now go through them one by one and imagine how your life would be without that characteristic. Don't move on to the next one until you've dealt completely with the previous one. The chances are that it will be difficult, though not impossible, to imagine, but that it will also evoke some strong feelings. We get very attached to these identities; in fact, we often imagine that they are all that we are. We are, however, more (or perhaps more aptly less) than this, and even without these characteristics we still are. We still exist. You may find that at the end of the exercise you have a sudden sense of the being that remains when all your special identities have been temporarily suspended!

This unique ability of human beings to reflect on existence and on ourselves makes us different from other animals and objects, but it comes at a price: that of personal responsibility.

The philosophical aims of existential therapy

Human issues were always the focus of Greek philosophy and the Greek myths are basically stories that explain how these issues can be understood and dealt with, rather like biblical stories also do. Greek philosophy (the word meaning 'love of wisdom') explored such issues more rationally and more effectively. It was indeed a search for wisdom about human existence that would lead us beyond mythology. Ultimately, existential therapy is a contemporary form of practical and applied philosophy that seeks to assist people in acquiring the wisdom to understand and live their lives with greater awareness and understanding. Therapy helps people do so through a process of judicious questioning and sifting through feelings, experiences and intuitions in order to come to clarity of reflection and insight.

The task of being human is not primarily psychological or biological but philosophical and the task of the existential therapist is to make this philosophical questioning practical and relevant to an individual's quest for a better life. The aim for the therapist is to work with the client in their search for truth with an open mind and an attitude of wonder, rather than fitting the client overtly or covertly into established frameworks of interpretation. It means that we have to be prepared to examine our assumptions about life.

The existential approach to therapy is about learning to philosophize in the sense of asking important questions about what it means to be alive. It places a responsibility on both the therapist and client to lucidly apply the ideas and to understand our position in the world and to evaluate the consequences in the light of truth and reality. When we do this wholeheartedly it becomes an enjoyable way of living life. Rather than seeking to minimize our difficulties, we learn to appreciate them as moments where we gain insight.

EXERCISE

Think of a time when you were mistaken about your evaluation of someone: let yourself think back to how this mistaken judgement came about, without judging yourself. Just observe the process of your own assumptions and prejudice.

- How do you jump to conclusions about other people?
- How do you decide whether something is right or true?
- What principles do you use to guide your decisions? Where do they come from?

It was Socrates and Plato who established this tradition of systematic thinking about human issues. Their aim was always one of helping people to live better lives in tune with sound principles and in search of the good and the true. Socrates gave his name to the process, the Socratic method, whereby the teacher acts as midwife, enabling pupils to give birth to their own understanding of the world. The philosophical teacher's discourse with the pupil was always cooperative and critical, following the virtues of orderliness, deliberateness and clarity. The teacher (therapist) and pupil (client) are both active and independent, though the teacher is able to offer experienced guidance.

It becomes clear when doing this, that it helps greatly to have expert guidance in reflecting on ourselves, especially when such reflection involves us having to face up to some of our own errors and mistaken prejudice. We need the extra pair of eyes to see more clearly. Of course, we can get some insights from studying on our own those philosophers who have thought about the complexities of human existence, but without another person present we are limited by the narrowness of our own vision.

KEY POINTS

- Existential philosophers are concerned with what it means to be alive.
- *That* we are is more fundamental than *what* we are.
- The search for truth that existential therapists engage in with their clients is handled like a philosophical research project that cannot be embarked on lightly and requires commitment and full engagement from both.
- While there is an ongoing search for models of living that can improve people's lives, there is no endorsement of any particular model.
- The existential counsellor will attempt to resonate with and articulate all aspects of the client's worldview.

- Clients will be encouraged to explore the polarities and paradoxes that underpin human living in general and their lives in particular.
- The process will consist of careful description of the client's experience and full exploration of its implications, reasons, purpose and consequences, and all interpretations must be verified.
- There is an awareness of the importance of dialogue and exchange of views, where each person is equal and capable of considering what can be learnt from the collaborative exploration.
- There has to be a willingness to test out hypotheses about human living and revise these in the light of new findings.

SOME OF THE MAJOR EXISTENTIAL PHILOSOPHERS

The following short biographies in chronological order give an idea of the diversity of existential thinking.

Søren Kierkegaard (1813–55) was a Danish philosopher who is sometimes called 'the father of existential thinking'. He wrote in an indirect manner often using pseudonyms and took issue with what he saw as the conformity of nineteenth-century bourgeois society and particularly with its hypocritical way of interpreting Christianity. He advocated learning from anxiety (Angst) and despair and he valued subjective truth over given truth. He believed that we all have to learn to live aesthetically first, then ethically, but that in order to learn to think for ourselves we need to dare to doubt, until we are able to make a leap of faith to find our own personal sense of and relationship to God.

Friedrich Nietzsche (1844–1900) was a German philosopher who wrote in a poetic and rhetorical manner and criticized what he called the herd mentality of his fellow citizens. An accomplished iconoclast, he opposed all systems especially value-laden ones. He is famous for stating that 'God is dead'. He said that each person must relentlessly question in order to aspire to a sense of truth and reality which goes beyond established values. We have to re-evaluate right and wrong and aspire to become what he called the *Übermensch*: the autonomous superhuman who creates his or her own values and morality, and lives a life of passion and personal affirmative power.

Edmund Husserl (1859–1938) was a logician and mathematician who designed a new method for describing and understanding all objects and acts of consciousness, including consciousness itself. He called this process 'phenomenology': the science of how things appear. He said that consciousness is always consciousness of something and can never be separated from its object. This is known as the principle of intentionality. Phenomenology is a procedure for

(Continued)

(Continued)

allowing us to become more aware of the various ways we prejudge physical, personal, social and ethical situations and to become able to grasp the essence of things directly, through the disciplined use of our intuition.

Martin Buber (1878–1965) was an Austrian Jewish philosopher and theologian. He emphasized that human existence was fundamentally relational. He proposed a distinction between 'I–Thou' and 'I–It' modes of relating, with the latter being more like our everyday relating to objects which is characterized by distance, partiality and exploitation. The former was based on a full and open appraisal and contact with the totality of the other. He described the importance of the space in between two people as it is co-created by them and so changes the quality of their interaction.

Karl Jaspers (1883–1969) was a German psychiatrist and a philosopher who, like Husserl, was dissatisfied with the ability of science to provide any insight into the human condition as we live it. He emphasized the permanent dilemma of the need for a 'worldview' in order not to despair at its absence, and the redemptive power of communication. He argued that it is in the unavoidable 'limit situations' like death, guilt, condemnation, doubt and failure that we are reminded of our existence. He also spoke of the importance of remaining aware of the comprehensive elements of our existence that transcend our everyday preoccupations.

Paul Tillich (1886–1965) was a German-born Protestant theologian who left for the United States in the 1930s. He advocated courage in the face of the anxiety of non-being, and distinguished between 'existential' and 'neurotic' anxiety. Tillich's notion of God is as a symbol of reality that we need to come to terms with in our everyday lives. He was a tutor to Rollo May, whose work he inspired.

Gabriel Marcel (1889–1973) was a French philosopher and playwright. He emphasized the basic mystery of existence, and the importance of openness to others, as well as the belief that to live properly requires one to have faith in the harmony for which human existence strives. He spoke of the fidelity to ourselves, to life and to each other and of the need to be prepared to be loyal whatever the future holds in store.

Martin Heidegger (1889–1976) was a German philosopher and is considered one of the most influential of the existential thinkers. His work emphasized the human capacity for resolute awareness, through engagement with the anxiety that is prompted by our awareness of our inevitable death. He also placed emphasis on what he called the ground of Being and argued that human beings had to be the guardians, or shepherds of being. He worked towards the end of his life with the Swiss psychiatrist Medard Boss and also influenced Ludwig Binswanger, a long-time colleague of Freud.

Jean-Paul Sartre (1905–80) was a French philosopher, novelist, playwright and political activist. Through his novels and plays he is probably the best-known existential philosopher. He is the person who coined the term 'existentialism' and is the only one who actively claimed to be an existentialist. He emphasized the nothingness at the core of existence that gives us freedom. He argued that most people try to escape this freedom and live in bad faith. He believed that to be free is to make choices and take responsibility as we define ourselves through our actions. We have no excuse not to define our life's project actively. He moved from a description of the competitive nature of human relations to a more collaborative model of human interaction.

Simone de Beauvoir (1908–86) was a philosopher who is primarily known for her feminist contribution and her novels which illustrate existential themes. She contributed groundbreaking work on issues of sexuality, gender and old age. She wrote about the ethics of freedom and contingency and spoke of the ambiguity of life and of the importance of being prepared to make new moral choices in each new situation.

Maurice Merleau-Ponty (1908–61) was a French philosopher and phenomenologist who emphasized the embodied nature of human existence. He highlighted the notion of intersubjectivity, which is the idea that there is no real separation between the self and the other. He showed how differently we can think of the world if we stop objectifying and separating ourselves from our experience, becoming aware of the intertwined ambiguity of all human experience.

Albert Camus (1913–60) was a French novelist and philosopher who, like de Beauvoir, is known for his novels. He emphasized that what makes life worthwhile is the struggle against what he called the absurdity, the basic meaninglessness of human existence. He argued that it is this engaged struggle itself that creates meaning.

LIMITS OF HUMAN LIVING: THE GIVENS OF EXISTENCE

One point all these authors agree on is that human life is finite and that this is the basic challenge we have to face. We are thrown into the world and have to accept the non-negotiable givens of our existence.

What we mean by 'thrown' is that certain facts of our existence are imposed upon us without any choice, for instance, our genetic make-up, family, gender, race and culture as well as the fact that we are born in the first place. We are thrown into a world that has given characteristics and limits. Our task is to make something of what we have been given. Complaining about not having been given a good enough hand of cards in life will achieve nothing. The hand we are born with is the hand we have to play.

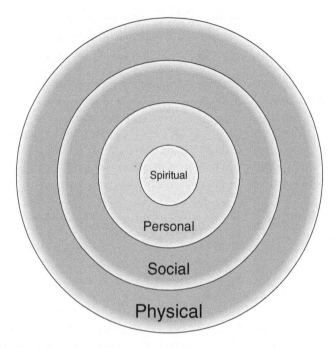

Figure 1.1   The Four dimensions of life

The four dimensions of existence

There is no existential personality theory which divides people into types or seeks to label them. Instead there is a description of the different dimensions of existence with which people from all cultures are confronted in various ways. These are the parameters of human existence.

The way a person is in the world at any particular time of their life can be charted on a general map of human existence (Binswanger, 1963; Yalom, 1980; Deurzen, 2010) which distinguishes four basic dimensions, or worlds of human existence. The four dimensions are represented in Figure 1.1 as concentric spheres. The outer layer represents the physical dimension; the layer below this covers the social dimension, followed by the inner space of the personal dimension with inside it the spiritual core. When we take a section of this sphere, it provides us with a map of the four dimensions of life. Of course, in reality, these realms of existence intertwine and intersect and are never as neatly arranged or separate from each other as this diagram would suggest. They intertwine in different ways for different people. It is a useful tool we can use in our practice to remind us not just of the simultaneous multidimensionality of existence but also of what aspects of their existence clients are currently talking about and, perhaps more importantly, what aspects they are not talking about. A map is simply something we can use to locate and orientate ourselves with. We must take care not to confuse the map for the territory.

Also known as the ultimate concerns, each dimension contains a challenge we engage with in different ways throughout our lives and which has the capacity to produce anxiety simply by virtue of it being unsolvable. The paradox is that engaging with it can lead to finding the necessary resolve and determination to overcome and transcend it.

Physical dimension

On the physical dimension (*Umwelt*), we relate to our environment and to the givens of the natural world around us. This is the outside ring of our world relations and includes the body we have, the concrete surroundings we find ourselves in, the climate and weather, objects and material possessions and our capacity for health and illness as well as our relationship to our own mortality.

The struggle on this dimension, in general terms, is between the search for domination over the elements and natural law, as in technology, or in sports, and the need to accept the limitations of natural boundaries, as in ecology or old age. While people generally aim for security on this dimension – through health and wealth, much of life brings a gradual disillusionment and realization that such security can only be temporary. Physical illnesses, both great and small, remind us of our mortal frailty.

The very early years of life are predominantly concerned with the physical, with survival; through satisfaction of bodily needs and physical safety. This is what love is about at this stage as well: providing physical comfort, satisfaction and security. Birth is the beginning of our physical existence, death is the end and our life is the space between. Often we return to this state in old age, of needing physical care and safety given to us by others. Paradoxically while everybody has a desire to live a long time, few of us wish to get old. Perhaps because we all know it will happen, we try not to think about it too much. We act as if we are immortal.

Although we know our death will come, we never know when or what it will be like. Most of us would agree with Woody Allen when he says, 'Death doesn't really worry me that much, I'm not frightened about it ... I just don't want to be there when it happens.'

When we say goodbye to a friend we say 'See you soon', with actually no more than a hope that there will be a 'soon'. Yet we have to find the courage to carry on as if there will be a 'soon'. We cannot literally choose to live forever, this is a function of genetics, the condition of our body, and chance, but what we can do is to choose our stance towards our life and this is intimately tied up with the way we see our death. In order to truly live, we all need to determine our relationship with death.

The paradox is that although physical death will kill me, the denial of death will destroy the time I have left but the idea of death will save me in the sense that it will prompt me to live my life more resourcefully and more fully.

The unsolvable dilemma is that mortality is a constant fact of our lives which we can either welcome or deny. We are reminded of it every time something comes to an end. The reality of present and future loss is inscribed in our hearts as much as our desire to postpone or avoid it. It is in the discovery of the physical constraints to existence that we discover the social world.

EXERCISE

Talk to a partner about one of these subjects for five minutes. Your partner just has to listen, not interrupt or ask you anything. Afterwards reflect on what it was like. Did you say what you intended to say?

- What was it like when you were or someone close to you was last ill?
- What was it like when you last had an accident that endangered your life?
- What things do you want to have done before you die?
- Describe yourself physically.

Social dimension

On the social dimension (*Mitwelt*), we relate to others and interact with the public world around us. This dimension includes our response to the culture we live in, as well as to the class and race we belong to and also those we do not belong to.

It is about the presence of other people in the world and the necessity of getting on with them. On the one hand, it sometimes seems easier not to have to deal with others, but, on the other, we need others for our physical and emotional survival and all too often we miss them, or feel lonely without them.

Sooner or later we are all confronted with aloneness and the knowledge that nobody can know what it is like to be me. Nevertheless I am aware that my past, my present and my future are bound up with other people and though we are all very much alike, each one of us is permanently separate from the other. And yet I know I need other people and I need to understand and be understood by other people. Every time we meet and separate from someone who matters to us this is brought home to us.

Each person has a separate body and a separate consciousness and we come up against others in conflict or cooperation. By acquiring fame or other forms of power, we can attain dominance over others, but only temporarily. The paradox therefore is that the awareness of my separateness can help me to understand and to respect the other.

The unsolvable dilemma is to do with our need for individuality combined with our need to be a part of a whole. Fusion and fission are the two inevitable poles of our relations to others.

EXERCISE

Talk to a partner about one of these subjects for five minutes. Your partner just has to listen, not interrupt or ask you anything. Afterwards reflect on what it was like. Did you say what you intended to say? Or did you surprise yourself?

- monogamy
- a relationship you have or had
- being on a desert island alone
- your social existence

Personal dimension

The relationship with oneself (*Eigenwelt*), is about having an inner world with views about one's character, past experience and future possibilities. People search for a feeling of being substantial and having a confident sense of self but life events remind us of personal weakness and can plunge us into confusion when we realize that things do not go the way we planned. Some people are confused about who they are.

We often act as if there is a rule book to life and look for it in different places, including going to counsellors or psychotherapists. Paradoxically it is only when we discover that there is no rule book that we become aware of the personal dimension. The possibility of this happening arises whenever we confront the unexpected, because it evokes anxiety which we then may seek to quell with distractions and prescribed or non-prescribed drugs until, after much evasion and denial, we discover that taking personal responsibility for making up our own mind is in fact the only way forward if we want to get a sense of being truly awake and in charge of our own life.

Sartre (2003) says that 'man is condemned to be free'. By 'condemned', he means that we cannot avoid freedom. The only choice we do not have is not to choose. Only when a person takes responsibility for their own choices can they truly learn about the consequences of their actions, their own authority and hence the meaning of their lives.

There are two ways to misunderstand responsibility: one is to take responsibility for things one has no responsibility for, and the other is to deny responsibility for things that one does have responsibility for. One or the other of these is the cause of most distress in life (apart from major disasters that strike us out of the blue).

This essential human freedom is the freedom to take responsibility *for* one's own actions. It is not a freedom *from* responsibility. A prerequisite for taking responsibility is that the person needs to acknowledge they are free within the constraints of reality to make decisions. What choice means to existential therapists is much more to do with commitment to a course of action. When one is free to choose and owns one's decision, one has earned the right to reap the benefits.

If being human was simply a process of cause and effect, there would be no such thing as creativity or imagination and all of life would be mechanical and predetermined.

The paradox is that when I realize I am weak and vulnerable and that there is no external rule book, I discover that in my freedom I can develop responsibility, stamina and personal strength. As long as I act as if I am invulnerable, I cannot come to terms with the vulnerability of being a person.

The unsolvable dilemma is that even as we make our choices we still look for some unchanging principles to live by.

EXERCISE

Talk to a partner about one of these subjects for five minutes. Your partner just has to listen, not interrupt or ask you anything. Afterwards reflect on what it was like. Did you say what you intended to say?

(Continued)

(Continued)

- What is the first thing that comes to mind when you think of the idea of freedom?
- Describe a recent time when things did not go the way you wished. How did it feel?
- Describe the last time you said 'I couldn't help it' or 'They made me do it'.
- Describe the last time you lied.
- Describe yourself personally.

Spiritual dimension

On the spiritual dimension (*Überwelt*), we relate to the unknown and thus create a sense of an ideal world and a personal value system. It is here that we find meaning and purpose through reflection.

The history of Western civilization over the past 500 years has gradually eroded our sense of specialness in the universe. First Copernicus and Galileo pointed out that the Earth was not the centre of the universe, but just one planet circling the sun. We discovered that there were many such solar systems and that the Earth was by no means at the centre of the universe. Then Darwin showed that we are just one of the many species evolving from the same gene pool by natural selection. Finally the work of theoretical physicists like Einstein and Heisenberg dismantled the notion of the objective certainty of knowledge and replaced it with one of ambiguity, relativity and intentionality. This parallels the findings of existential philosophers who argued for a fresh approach to living in the face of the new information we have obtained about the world. In the sense that life is about meaning creating, the spiritual dimension is the central axis of existential therapy.

We cannot help but have certain beliefs and ideas about how everything in life fits together. This is our worldview. It orientates us in the world, defines our attitude towards it and allows us to create meaning. Our value system gives us a sense of right and wrong and enables us to succeed in what the Greeks called 'living the good life'. We like to believe that this is absolute or 'god-given' – that the principles are for all time. But we encounter numerous obstacles that make us feel like giving up and come to realize that the value system we live by is defined by us and us alone. And it is not absolute. This is what is meant by absurdity. Meaninglessness and absurdity are common experiences and most of us fear these so much that we would do anything to avoid them.

For some people this is done through a prescriptive worldview like the dogma of a religion, for others, it is more personal. People create their values in terms of something that matters enough to live or die for, something that may even be ultimately and universally valid. Usually the aim is something that will surpass human mortality like having contributed something valuable to mankind. Instant celebrity can be seen as an easy but flawed way to immortality.

Facing the void and the possibility of nothingness are the indispensable counterparts of this quest for the eternal. The contradictions that have to be faced on this dimension are related to the tension between purpose and absurdity, hope and despair.

EXERCISE

Talk to a partner about one of these subjects for five minutes. Your partner just has to listen, not interrupt or ask you anything. Afterwards reflect on what it was like. Did you say what you intended to say?

- A time when I was not treated the way I wanted by someone.
- My parents' values: those I have adopted and those I baulk at.
- Something I used to believe, but no longer hold to.
- Who I would like to write a thank you letter to or receive one from and why.
- Exploring my views on specific beliefs I have about what happens after death.
- Describe yourself spiritually.

An existential view of religion

Existential philosophers such as Buber and Tillich explored the religious dimension of human life, and some others like Nietzsche and Sartre argued vigorously against it. People often say that God is looking over them and supporting them and that they feel connected to something greater than themselves. Other people are agnostic or atheistic. Whatever we believe is compatible with an existential exploration of spirituality. It is important to know how people conceived of their connection to a reality greater than themselves, be this society, being, the universe, a god or the principle of love. People for whom this basic trust in transcendence is absent will feel as if they are not watched over or safe. They may even feel abandoned or persecuted and try to control events. They are out of touch with the way in which they are connected to the world – what Heidegger meant by being-in-the-world. We are always a constituent part of our own and also of other people's world. Therefore there is neither a force 'out there' nor 'in here', but within us and without us at the same time. We are both/ and: separate and yet connected.

Such a force or principle of connectivity is not an interventionistic entity. It just is. Existentially this has to be trusted, and if we can trust ourselves and others and accept our collective dynamic uncertainty, we will be able to take advantage of the chances and opportunities that life offers and we will also be able to take responsibility for these. Alcoholics Anonymous was founded on the insight that the spiritual dimension was lacking in the lives of addicts. AA is rejected by some addicts who are threatened by what they wrongly see as the foundation of AA on religious dogma. In fact, it is founded on the idea of connectedness and trust in self and others. This is the existential meaning of the spiritual.

The paradox is that realizing that there is no grand design prompts us to engage more resiliently with our own life and spurs us on to make our own ethical system in order to make our lives meaningful.

The unsolvable dilemma is that our need for ultimate meaning and purpose persists even as we come to accept the relativity of our existence.

KEY POINTS

- We live simultaneously on four different dimensions: the physical, the social, the psychological and the spiritual.
- Each of these set us different dilemmas and challenges which can only ever be temporarily solved.
- If we do not acknowledge the influence and importance of all the dimensions, our lives will become unbalanced.

LIVING IN TIME

Existentially we think of time as having two dimensions. There is clock time, which, as the name suggests, is measured by the clock, is regular and linear. One minute follows the previous at the same rate and will always do so.

Then there is existential time, and it is more accurate to say that we are temporal, we are in time. It is a defining quality of our existence that we are born, and that we will die. We move in a perpetually changing present with our past behind and future ahead of us. In this sense, the past and future are contained within the present. When we talk about the present, we mean a present that contains all that has happened and all that will happen. Past and future meet in the present. Our task in understanding this is to realize that the way we are is not determined by the past, for the past can change. A simple example of this is that when we are happy we find it easier to remember happy times we have had, and similarly with sad times. Letting go of the idea that we are determined by the past gives us freedom but also brings the responsibility to change. If anything, the future is primary because we are always aware of the certainty of death and the problem of how to live a meaningful life before we die.

KEY POINTS

- The present includes the past and the future.
- Understanding that we are not determined is to realize that we can own our past and future and not to feel it is imposed upon us. So we become active creators of our lives and not passive recipients of it.

LIVING WITH PARADOX

All life's paradoxes are related to one or more of the four dimensions of existence and clients often try to solve them with an either/or decision. Most problem-solving techniques involve this. But deciding between alternatives such as: 'Should I do this or should I do that?' cannot be solved by rhetoric or by argument. Rhetoric is useful where certainty is desirable, facts are clear and solutions seem permanent. Dialectical decision-making is usually more appropriate in relation to human issues, which are not mechanical but are about understanding, processing and finally a personal commitment to a course of action.

In dialectics, an initial statement – or thesis – 'should I do this...?' – gives rise to a counter-statement – or antithesis – 'or that?'– and the opposition between the two is resolved by something which contains elements of both, but is different from either. This synthesis then becomes a new thesis, and so on. For Socrates, it was a means of overcoming opposites through dialogue in order to get closer to the truth.

Existential therapy proceeds by dialectically facing up to conflict and polarity, learning to tolerate ambiguity and the unexpected in order to arrive at a synthesis which, because of the dynamic nature of existence, is always temporary and provisional.

Life in fact is given its excitement by this ambiguity and if we are able to take the paradoxes of existence in our stride and tolerate the anxiety that comes with the freedom of the both/and, we are more likely to live a satisfying life.

Table 1.1 presents the paradoxes that regularly confront us. It is only if we face the basic challenge at each level that we gain new strength. If we try to avoid it, we lose more than we gain.

TABLE 1.1   THE PARADOXES OF HUMAN EXISTENCE

	Challenge to face up to	Potential gain	Potential loss
Physical	Death	Living life to the full	An unlived life or constant fear
Social	Separateness and loneliness	To understand and to be understood	Bullying or being bullied; dependency
Personal	Vulnerability and weakness	Discovering stamina and strength	Egocentricity, narcissism and self-destructiveness
Spiritual	Meaninglessness	Evolving a system of ethics to live by	Fanaticism, fundamentalism apathy

KEY POINTS

- Life is a mystery to be lived, not a problem to be solved.
- Paradoxes can only be approached in a both/and way and also can never be solved once and for all.
- We have to be willing to face up to our troubles.

ANXIETY AND THE GIVENS OF EXISTENCE

Awareness of these givens of existence gives rise to what existential philosophers call Anxiety, Angst, Ontological Anxiety or Existential Anxiety. Anxiety in this sense is spelt with a capital 'A', to distinguish it from the more familiar everyday experience of anxiety with a small 'a'. It is a theoretical concept and no one feels Anxiety as such. Instead each everyday anxiety or worry we have, great and small, can be related back to one or more of the basic paradoxes. Since these can never be removed, only evaded or denied, the task of life is to appreciate, understand and live with them. Heidegger says that if we move too far away from our anxieties about the facts of life, we are drawn back to them by the 'call of conscience'. To live is to never be completely safe and it is this engagement with the paradoxes and dilemmas of living that gives human existence its excitement and sense of aliveness. It is in this tension that we find the source of all true creativity. Anxiety is a teacher, not an obstacle or something to be removed or avoided.

Humanistic psychology talks about the person being drawn to achieve their potential as if there were a force for good that moves the person forwards, like a seed that seeks to expand and grow. The existential view is rather different. The paradoxes and dilemmas of each of the four dimensions give boundaries to our lives and the tension thus created motivates people in various ways to explore the space within the boundaries. Growth is not necessarily positive and change is not always for the better. We have to open our eyes to the various possibilities and dangers that exist, and choose our path. Existence is created out of this and without our continuous aspirations and desperations, ups and downs, attachments and losses, there would be no human meaning.

KEY POINT

- Anxiety pervades all aspects of existence and engaging rather than evading or denying it gives life its excitement and meaning.

THE MIND AND THE BODY

Contemporary thinking encourages us to believe not just that the body is separate from the world, but also that the mind is separate from the body. But it is just as difficult to imagine a body without a mind as it is to imagine a mind without a body.

We get into this muddle because we have displaced our attention from our experience as embodied beings into the abstract notion of an independent material body which behaves like a machine, but has sensations, thoughts and feelings, within.

Existential therapists do not accept a functional distinction between the mind, the body and the world, preferring to think of the human being as an embodied consciousness that is able to reflect upon itself always in a context.

In fact, the most fundamental mode of interaction we have is with the world. Our identity, the way we think about ourselves is inseparable from the world. Our worldview is literally the view of the world from here, from and including this body. It is not just the perspective we have on the world, it is the way we experience and interpret the world we are a part of.

It is not simply cognitive but more like an atmosphere we both absorb and exude. In fact, we take it so much for granted we are often unaware of our particular way of perceiving the world. In art, perspective refers to both a view of the world and to the view of the world from *here*.

The nature of our body dictates the nature of our worldview. The rise of technology has contributed to this separation of the body from the world. Until the late nineteenth century, the beginning of the scientific age, all measurements were made in terms of the body, for example, an inch was the width of a thumb, a foot was the length of an adult foot and a furlong, a furrow-long, was how far a ploughing team could be driven without resting. Everyone knew this. With the advent of standardized and objective measures this connection to the body has been lost.

There are many phrases that we use, often without thinking, that refer to the way we interact with the world through our body. We talk about someone being a 'pain in the neck'. We refer to someone's weak point as their 'Achilles' heel', from the Greek myth. When we feel confident, we talk about feeling 'grounded'. When we are happy, we feel 'light'. When we are depressed, we feel 'heavy'.

As children we experience settings like playgrounds as large and when we return to them as adults we are surprised to find that they are not as large as we remember. They only seemed large because we were small. People smaller than average often dislike crowds because they literally cannot see their way out. For anyone who loses their mobility, the world becomes a different place, somewhere they cannot inhabit with the same freedom.

Quite often we think in terms of whether our body is acceptable by societal norms. We think about it as an 'it', an object of approval or disapproval. This makes the body, and indeed our self, into a possession or a thing. In contemporary culture the human being is in danger of becoming standardized.

Existential therapists consider that the body is not something we have. It is what we are. Nietzsche talks about the 'intelligent body' in the sense that we need to listen to the body and to be at one with the body. When we lose this ability to listen, we involve ourselves in destructive activities. We see this most characteristically in people with eating disorders who have lost or somehow learnt to deny the ability to know whether they are hungry or not. Food or its absence is then used to separate the person from the message of their body and food and its consequences take on another meaning for a person, much more to do with their acceptability as human beings or their relationship to a depriving or stifling world. Consequently they eat when they are not hungry or do not eat when they are hungry in an attempt to gain some balance.

Moreover, focussing on intake of food becomes a means of finding distraction from the paradoxes and dilemmas of existence. Focussing on the appearance of the body and its shortcomings is seen in its most extreme form as Body Dysmorphic Disorder, where people end up having an erroneous sense of their body shape.

The philosopher Gilbert Ryle (1949) described the problem as a 'category error', because the mind is not a thing at all and therefore is not fixed, and we should not be talking about 'the mind' but of the process of 'minding'. We have to remember that mind is a verb, not a noun.

EXERCISE

Find a quiet space on your own and sit as comfortably as you can, shut your eyes and scan through your body starting with your toes and describe each part of your body to yourself. Don't hurry and move through your body slowly, giving enough time to each part. What was it like?

Now find a partner to do the same thing with. Sit facing each other a few feet apart with your eyes shut and go through your body as before. What difference does it make for both of you to do it in the presence of the other?

Now with the same partner sit opposite each other, and look at each other without talking, moving your eyes over the other's body stopping on parts you wish to stop on, for 5 minutes. What was it like?

KEY POINTS

- Neither the mind nor the body are things that we have, they are things that we are – they are inseparable aspects of our being.
- Being-in-the-world refers to the way we are always making and being made by the world around us. We are inseparable from the world.

2

THE PERSON OF THE THERAPIST

Know thyself.

The Temple of Apollo, Delphi

WHO ARE YOU?

Existential psychotherapy is a relationship between two people. It is not technical or mechanical, but an encounter, a meeting of souls. In this meeting each person is just as important as the other. In existential therapy we start with the therapist, and train them to be capable of using themselves purposefully and well in the therapeutic relationship. It is important to begin by understanding the kind of person you are. Your motivation for doing the job and your capacity for learning are paramount. It is impossible to be a good existential therapist unless you have the willingness and ability to look into yourself before you look into other people's lives. This is an ethical and practical principle. But a willingness to know yourself is not enough. You must also be prepared to face up to life's complexity and grapple with the paradoxes and difficulties described in Chapter 1.

The necessity for a person to make sense of their own life is at the centre of existential philosophy and practice. The existential therapist will know something about not just how to make sense of things but, even more anxiety-provoking, they will know that the sense they make will only be provisional, temporary.

THE USE OF LIFE EXPERIENCE TO REFLECT ON LIFE AND ITS MEANINGS

What makes us special as human beings is our ability to reflect on our past, present and also our future and this ability to understand life experience in the physical, social, personal and spiritual dimensions will contribute to our ability to monitor ourselves for personal bias. Clients are entitled to have a therapist who has grappled with the issues and questions that life raises.

Although reflecting is something we do automatically, our conclusions are often mistaken either because they are so familiar and we think of them as normal, or because we would rather not examine them too closely because they evoke anxiety.

The many ways we deceive ourselves about our experience and our personal responsibility by restricting our worldview is something we need to be alive to. Existential therapists are likely to be people who have always spent time thinking about the world and their place in it. They are likely to have experimented and travelled and are certain to have been curious about other people and about their own motivations. In order to refine their understanding of all these things, they will have gone through a phase of reflection on life and their own conduct, their personal worldview, values and bias in one-to-one existential therapy. This allows them to fine-tune their vision about themselves and tune out any huge prejudices, presumptions and fears that might interfere with their clear perception of others. Supervision is a way of formalizing this professionally and continuing a process of self and life scrutiny during and after training.

We tend to think that maturity comes with age but existential maturity does not come automatically with age because some younger people may have weathered greater storms and lived their relatively shorter lives with greater intensity than their elders and will therefore have understood more about existence and have matured into fuller human beings.

The sort of maturity that is required for existential therapists will show itself in an ability to make room for all sorts of, even contradictory, opinions, attitudes, feelings, thoughts and experiences and to have the ability to integrate these into the person you are. You will have the ability to be uncertain, to feel that you do not have to know the answers to problems though you will keep searching.

Rather than clinging to one point of view, existential therapists will be able to oversee and evaluate reality from a range of perspectives and will have the ability to distinguish truth from lies as well as knowing when to be unsure. They will be able to tolerate the tension that awareness of such contradictions generates.

There are a number of life experiences that are particularly helpful in preparing people for such maturation:

- Committing oneself to raising a family, or caring for dependants in a close relationship is instrumental in creating an open attitude and discovering the nature of love.
- Becoming a parent or a step-parent enables a person to see life from the point of view of a father or mother as well as a son or daughter. This can help people understand both how rewarding and also how difficult parenting can be. Many women have little academic schooling but great practical experience in this area. This may be the same for men who have taken responsibility for child care.
- Being immersed in society from several angles, in different jobs, different academic studies, different social classes, and so on, is a definite advantage.
- Cross-cultural experience is also an excellent way to stretch the mind and one's views on what it means to be human. Spending some time living in another country is a

good way to appreciate that there are different ways of living. People who have had to adjust their way of perceiving and dealing with the world, especially when this includes a change of language, have had the all-important experience of questioning previous assumptions and opening up to a new culture and perspective.

- People coming to psychotherapy as a second career are often especially suitable because they have had the experience of wishing to change their life direction and also having the courage to make the change.
- The sine qua non of becoming an existential therapist is to have negotiated a number of significant crossroads in one's personal life. Nothing opens a person more to the mysteries and possibilities of being than to witness birth, suffering and death.
- Many existential therapists have first awoken to their interest in human difficulties and the vagaries of life when they were confronted with a crisis in their own life. Far from adversity being a negative, it is the condition for the kind of mellowing and maturing that is required of someone who takes the role of therapist and facilitator of life understanding.

EXERCISE

Take a few minutes to write down for yourself what you think has been a significant experience of existential crisis, in which you initially thought you might
flounder and lose your foothold in reality, but then discovered that you were able
to let yourself be transformed and transfigured by it instead. How did you let
yourself trust the experience and how were you able to let it help you to bend
rather than break? What of this experience will help you be a therapist?

The moral stance that existential therapists take is that they would not expect clients to commit to greater depth and intensity than they are prepared to commit to themselves. Therefore trainees need to commit to a therapy of their own in which they take the opportunity to plumb the depth of their own heart and soul and come to terms with their own conflicts and contradictions. An existential therapist will actively engage with such personal therapy to find out its possibilities and limitations and know for themselves the doubts that need to be faced and the premises that need to be explored.

Existential therapists will have been able to develop their ability to deal with their share of existential crises so that their own lives are enriched rather than impoverished by the experience. In therapy, they will absorb such experiences and pluck the fruits of their learning, harvesting and storing the wisdom they hold.

KEY POINTS

- Although effective existential therapists will be skilful practitioners, it is more important that they have the ability to learn from life experience.
- Continuing to live reflectively and with awareness is the best way of becoming a good existential therapist.

BEING-WITH: RECIPROCITY, COLLABORATION AND TRUST

As we saw in Chapter 1, human beings are always in relation to others as well as in relation to things, themselves and ideas. Sartre pointed out that there are two ways to be with others, competitively or cooperatively. And there are three ways of being competitive:

- We can aim for *dominance*, controlling or subjecting the other and fighting when this does not work. In this case, relationships are seen as something to 'win at'.
- We can aim to be *submissive*, letting ourselves be controlled, placating the other, often trying to soothe them or meet their needs at the exclusion of our own. In this case, we see relationships as something to 'lose at' or 'suffer in'.
- We can merely *withdraw* from all relationships, refusing to 'play the game'. We can withhold affection and pretend we do not value the company of others. This is usually the last move in a competitive game in which we feel hopelessly inadequate and have been hurt too much to try again.

Cooperative relationships, on the contrary, are relationships in which we dare to put ourselves at the disposal of the creation of something of value. We work together and we respect each other's needs without feeling obliged to meet them. Such relationships are characterized by the following traits:

- We feel we are able to give generously without counting the cost, for we have faith that the other will do likewise.
- We are constantly exploring the differences and similarities between us and make room for the complementarity this affords: we make the most of the additional strength we get from each other.
- We work with an unwritten rule of reciprocity: we are aware that we cannot just take over shared space and time but need to mind both our own and the other's needs and be equitable in dividing up available resources.
- We seek to proceed on a collaborative basis, where each does as much as they can, putting their talents at the disposal of the couple, or group, to the best of their ability, rather than in an attempt to rival or compete with others and while gratefully receiving other contributions as well.

Clearly cooperative relationships can never be taken for granted and are for ever at risk of becoming competitive as soon as one or all partners in the relationship feel short-changed or overpowered or outsmarted and therefore threatened in their safety rather than upheld by each other. In existential couple or group therapy, such matters need to be carefully monitored, so that partners or participants are able to get back in touch with their own ability to thrive on being with others rather than become trapped in the vagaries of competitiveness.

EXERCISE

Reflect on these questions:

- Are you competitive or cooperative?
- Do you tend to engage in competition or do you tend to avoid it?
- What is it like to win?
- What is it like to lose?
- What is your earliest memory of winning and losing?

Now ask someone who knows you very well, what their experience of you is.

As therapists, we need to learn how to be with others in a cooperative rather than a competitive way, otherwise we cannot be fully available to our clients. But of course we need to be capable to stand firm and to face conflict as well. Being a therapist is not just about being positive, caring and empathic.

There often is confusion about the role of empathy in existential work. It was the existential philosopher Jaspers who first promoted the idea of empathy, as a way of 'feeling into' another's experience. He said that therapists need to dare to participate in the client's experience, resonating with it as fully as they can. While we can never feel what the client is feeling, what we can do is to take their experience into our selves and engage and resonate with it. That this is not foolproof is frequently evident when we discover that what we thought our clients meant has not been fully understood and was more to do with our own experience. Our capacity for resonance has to be honed constantly. It requires us to be fully present: co-present with the other and to take part in the therapeutic encounter as a fully engaged human being. Once we have let ourselves be affected by the other's experience of the world, we can hear and understand them inwardly, from the depth of our own experience. This will give us a much sharper perspective on the issues they bring, not by identifying, sympathizing or even empathizing with the other, but rather by applying the reality of the other's existence to ourselves in a real and truthful way. We do not do this in order to solve the other's problem for them, by jumping in for them, but to get the philosophical sense and deeply felt experience of the situation that provides us with the long view. From here we can jump ahead for them and so reveal the totality of the experience. Of course this has to be done carefully and gently and with great attention to the relationship that is evolving.

It is a given that relationships are difficult. It is what clients come to talk about most and they are difficult because of our co-constituted nature, the fact that we are both individual and together. Even a hermit is aware of the absence of others and his identity is as a person-without-others. We are defined by the way in which others relate to us and the way in which we relate to others. In the contemporary world of constant personal and electronic communication there is no way in which we can escape from each other.

Existential therapy emphasizes the cooperative nature of the work and this goes for the therapist's relationships outside the consulting room as well as for those inside because if a person is not able to do it in daily life, it is unlikely they will be able to do it as therapists.

Existential therapists will have a clear knowledge from their own experience of what can go wrong in relationships but perhaps more importantly what can go right, and also what they can do to make one into the other and how to tell the difference. They will know that trust will not grow without risk and without being tested. They will have learnt to judge when a situation can be trusted and when it cannot.

Although it may not seem obvious, it is important to know that gaining and losing trust is active rather than passive. Very simply, trust is gained by being consistent and doing what we say we will do at the time we promised. Mistrust comes out of our disappointment when people are not true to their word or circumstances do not meet our expectations.

This reflects directly on our work as therapists because our clients trust us when they dare to risk telling us something that is important and find out it is treated with respect, interest and understanding. It creates a new sense of hope for them. The principle of trust building is the glue that maintains and deepens relationships and one's sense of belonging.

In therapy, we must remember that although reciprocal, the relationship is not equal. The therapist and client are there for different purposes and are in different roles. Many of the breaches of ethics acted on by professional organizations are because of therapists mistakenly seeing reciprocity as meaning equality. Because clients come to therapists in a vulnerable position, we need to respect this and not expect them to respond as vigorously to our interventions as a friend or partner would. We need to give them the leeway to explore themselves without having to defend themselves from us.

The personal and the political

Being-with is not just about close relationships; it has a political dimension too. We have an inbuilt capacity to form groups and all groups need rules to operate by. The existential therapist will therefore understand their reciprocal relationship with the world and will often take an active part in political life, whether professional, community or party politics.

The personal is intertwined with the political and most of Sartre's plays explore this relationship. For people to be able to change for the better they need to know that the world around them will have a chance of changing for the better too. We are interlinked with our social environment and are as much influenced by it as we can influence it in turn.

Many people have criticized the political stances of Heidegger and Sartre among others, and Heidegger's Nazi affiliation with particularly good reason, but what is not in doubt is that these philosophers were deeply engaged politically and dared to live their lives in accordance with their own beliefs. In doing so, they made mistakes.

It is a part of our responsibility as a member of a community to vote in elections and this is one of the practical meanings of being-in-the-world, of living existentially.

Some people may, of course, opt for abstention from this process and set themselves apart from society. This needs to be understood in terms of what it means to the person who gives up belonging to the wider world of society or who gives up having an effect on it.

KEY POINTS

- Respecting someone's autonomy means to be able to accept them because of their differences rather than in spite of them.
- Without reciprocity and cooperation, the fabric of society will collapse and we will lose our individual and collective humanity and identity.
- Existential therapists explore personal, social, cultural and political relationships in equal measure.

CAPACITY FOR SELF-RELIANCE AND INDIVIDUALITY

In order to feel at ease in their personal world, people seek self-reliance. What is less obvious is that they will only acquire self-reliance through engagement with their own struggles in life. True self-reliance will mean that the person can be happy to be in their own company, and also that they are able to enjoy deeper personal relations with close friends and family members, rather than more shallow relationships with many people. This is another example of the both/and. The closer we are to ourselves, the more we are at ease in intimate relationships.

This results in being more able to judge which relationships will be mutually nourishing and to know how to make them deeper and more trusting. This cannot be done without understanding that being autonomous does not mean being a loner, and it also does not mean simply reacting against what others believe. It means freeing oneself to be part of a group without losing one's sense of self. People who can do this may seem at first glance to be quite ordinary people but they will have worked out not just what they believe, but also how to work out what to believe in unexpected situations. They are independent but not isolated. They are, in fact, nonconformists in the best sense.

Often they will have an ability to see something as if they've never seen it before. This is what it means to be phenomenological and although it may come across as ignorance or naivety, it is in fact openness and an ability to tolerate uncertainty.

Another aspect of self-reliance and individuality is that financial independence, the ability to look after oneself materially, to work, and to live within one's means, is a characteristic of healthy living. They will also know that financial independence is something valuable for the client to strive towards. Although often not given much importance in therapy, it is equivalent in importance to becoming reliable and trustworthy in human relationships.

Humour

Humour can be used to connect or to distance. Therapists' sense of humour will not be used to distance, confuse or put down and it will not be tinged with bitterness, contempt or cynicism. The existential therapist's sense of humour will be used sparingly and often to emphasize the irony and tragedy of existence which they are a part of. If clients feel that they are being made fun of or their issue is being made light of, the therapy will be undermined and trust will be lost.

KEY POINTS

- Self-reliance means being able to value your own company as well as that of others.
- Self-reliance comes from learning to trust your own ability to look after yourself and share with others.

TRANSPARENCY AND WISDOM

Other therapeutic perspectives do not systematically accommodate people's experience of the sacred or the spiritual. When we talk about transparency, we refer to the spiritual dimension of existence and the ability to see all the parts of life as connected and equally significant. Transparency requires us to be open to our inner thoughts, feelings, sensations and intuitions, and also to the facts of life. To be prepared to face truth, no matter what it is or what it leads us to. This takes humility and courage.

In everyday life we all struggle with opposing forces of good and evil, meaning and meaninglessness and often take cover by opting for one side or the other or by dodging or fudging the issue entirely. The principle of transparency, which consists of making ourselves available to all that is, can guide our search for truth. It demands that we no longer see ourselves as the centre of the universe, but as part of a greater complexity to which we belong and owe our lives. This is by no means easy because it involves abandoning some beliefs that give the illusion of safety. It is easy to say clichés like 'life is what you make it' or 'it takes all sorts to make a world', and these are no less true for being clichés, but they are much harder to actually live by. People who say them a lot are more likely to be trying to persuade themselves or others than accepting and opening themselves to what is the case. Phrases of this sort in therapy are likely to shut down an examination of the mystery of life.

Transparency and wisdom also relate to how existential thinkers see the 'self' not as a thing but as a process. Using the metaphor of the eye, much Western thinking as reflected in psychotherapy theories sees the self as something relatively fixed and internal that is illuminated when light comes in. Existentially, the self is much more like the iris of the eye that lets in the light of existence. The metaphor of sight is not about looking at the world, it is about letting the world in and being connected to it.

When we open our metaphorical 'iris', we are able to 'see' the world clearly and transparently, in its multidimensional glory and we are also able to see our place in it and what we can contribute to it. We have to aspire to be as transparent and open as possible so that 'light', existence, can shine in. When this happens, the person can simultaneously and reciprocally be lit up and light up the world.

This is what it means to be a part of the world, to be-in-the-world. From this position of being a part of the world while also being of it and being for it, we can contemplate human existence in a much more philosophical manner. We gain perspective on what truly matters and what is incidental.

EXERCISE

Transparency and wisdom could hardly be put better than by the social and ethical philosopher Reinhold Niebuhr (1892–1971) who asked us to have: 'the serenity to accept the things we cannot change, the courage to change the things we can and the wisdom to know the difference'.

Think of something in your current life that you want to change and something you want to learn to accept will remain the same.

KEY POINTS

- Human beings are able to choose when to be open and connected or closed and disconnected.
- It is the active reaching for truth that gives life its meaning, not the finding.

WHO ARE YOU AS A THERAPIST?

Working as an existential therapist makes particular demands on the person. The necessity for a person to know how to make sense of their own life is at the centre of existential philosophy and practice and the person will need to be able to make full use of their available personal and professional resources in order to function as an existential therapist.

Surviving as an existential psychotherapist

Being an existential psychotherapist can be a lonely job and private practice can make it even lonelier if it leads to a reduced social world, and we need to know what to do in order to survive as a therapist and as a person, for existentially the two are indivisible.

Many existential psychotherapists come to the work from another profession. This is always valuable since it means they have a broader view of human existence. But in order to be effective they need to continue having other interests and commitments in their lives.

If a therapist cannot do this, they will find that they are using their clients to meet the needs that their own interests and personal relationships should meet. For the short time we meet our clients they have an absolute right to our full attention but they also need to be assured, though not necessarily explicitly, that we have a productive and stimulating life outside the consulting room. Many existential psychotherapists maintain a parallel career in a separate but related field and this enhances rather than dilutes their work as therapists. Also it seems that a comparatively large number of existential therapists are also active in the arts. This too can only enhance their work as therapists.

In case all this sounds too idealistic, existential therapists are aware that they are first and foremost human beings and are therefore susceptible to human flaws, imperfections, blind spots, conflicts and dilemmas. They are familiar with feelings like anxiety, guilt, distress, joy and sadness but there is also a likelihood that they may understand how these things are part and parcel of being alive and that it is possible to make sense of them and that therapists diminish themselves if they try to eliminate them.

Supervision has a part to play but more important to survival is the ability to monitor ourselves for personal bias and hence to learn from experience. It is about knowing when we are functioning below par and when we need a break.

KEY POINTS

- We all need a time to forget there is such a thing as existential psychotherapy.
- We can only help others to live full lives if we live a full life ourselves.

THE IMPORTANCE OF PERSONAL THERAPY IN YOUR TRAINING

The issue of the place of personal therapy as a part of training has a particular meaning for existential therapists. There can be no doubt that to be an existential therapist you have to be prepared to scrutinize yourself and to learn as much about living as is possible. It is not sufficient simply to experience life, you have to systematically reflect on it and learn from ongoing experience as well. To have a special mentor, in the form of a therapist, with whom you can discuss your own questions about life and your own role in it, is just as necessary as to study the philosophers, psychologists and novelists who have created the ideas and theories that help us to understand human nature and the human condition. While we learn a great deal about how to be a therapist from our experience as a client, it is also necessary to learn essential skills in sessions of practical training and then to practise these in a wide variety of contexts and with many different clients under supervision.

KEY POINTS

- Existential training involves becoming familiar with both philosophical and psychological theories.
- It also involves skills training and supervised practice.

- An existential analysis requires active reflection on your life experience.
- Therapy for you as a therapist is about taking the time to learn about your life in a disciplined way.

HOW TO USE SUPERVISION?

Existential therapists set great stock by supervision. Supervision is interpreted as being literally about learning to oversee the whole of one's professional interactions to gain a better perspective on them. Supervision is a collaborative process and not a prescriptive or punitive exercise. Of course, supervision will be different during training than after qualification, when it may become a peer experience, either in one-to-one situations or in a group or both. Supervision is a joint search for the truth of human existence, by taking a wider view of the client's predicaments and taking a more careful and moderated account of their experiences. The supervisor will inevitably have a different experience and usually a greater level of experience from the supervisee, and this will help focus on many different aspects of the therapeutic relationship. This will include aspects of supervision that other approaches would also bring, such as a better understanding of the client's past, internal world and relationships, including the therapeutic relationship. But the existential extra is to add a bird's eye view of existence and the human condition, allowing for a broader perspective to emerge, which often makes for a valuable change from other forms of therapeutic supervision (Figure 2.1 from Deurzen and Young, 2009).

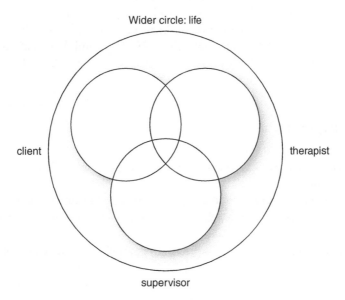

Figure 2.1 Existential aspects of supervision

Existential supervision focuses on many different levels and widens the supervisee's awareness of the following:

- the client's own world and daily way of being;
- the client's interrelations with others and the impact of those others on them;
- the client's values, beliefs, assumptions and aspirations;
- the therapist's own personal world, way of being, beliefs, values and convictions, including their unspoken projects and aspirations for the client's potential change and improvement;
- the relationship between client and therapist;
- the process of the therapy itself;
- what goes on between supervisor and therapist in the supervision session;
- sometimes it will particularly look at how this supervisory relationship may mirror the relationship between client and therapist as well as that between the client and other people in their life (parallel process);
- it will also look at how the client's way of being foregrounds the issues that the client is preoccupied with and tries to understand and make sense of these;
- it will look at the therapist's understanding of what the client says, does and experiences and look for connections between their lives, both in terms of similarities and differences;
- it will enable the therapist to put themselves in the client's place and feel into the client's world;
- it will sometimes concentrate on the therapeutic relationship seeking to enhance the interactions and interventions the therapist might make;
- it will occasionally speculate about other ways of being that might be available to the client, only to return to the main idea, which is to help the client to learn to be attentive to who they are and learn to just be themselves;
- most importantly it will consider the human and philosophical problems and issues brought forward by the client, implicitly or explicitly and illuminate these so as to expand the horizon of both client and therapist and grapple with the tasks and challenges of human living.

KEY POINTS

- Existential supervision starts from the experience of the therapeutic relationship.
- The existential supervisor will always acknowledge the autonomy of the therapist while at the same time taking responsibility for their own autonomy and knowledge.
- Existential supervision is a collaborative search for the truth of human existence.

3

WORKING PHENOMENOLOGICALLY: THE CENTRE OF EXISTENTIAL THERAPY

We are what we think. All that we are arises with our thoughts. With our thoughts, we make the world.

Buddha

Phenomenology aims to clarify the assumptions we make about the world and our part in it in order that we may see ourselves, the world and our relationship with it more clearly. When we work phenomenologically with clients, they discover how to separate true beliefs from false beliefs.

PHENOMENOLOGY: ASSUMPTIONS, BIASES, BLIND SPOTS AND THE WORLDVIEW

Any investigation, and therapy is an investigation, needs a method which will produce reliable findings. The physical sciences all use the natural scientific method. It works very well with inanimate objects, which have an essence, but does not work so well with people, because they are capable of choice and constant transformation.

A method that works a bit better with people is introspection, because it captures an individual's subjective activity. What is lost in introspection, however, is objectivity. There is no alternative point of view. Clients come to therapy because they are unable to come up with viable alternative points of view about their issues and the therapist is there to provide this new perspective.

Neither objective science nor subjective introspection are appropriate for human research, and so in the early twentieth century Edmund Husserl devised phenomenology as a disciplined method more appropriate for the human sciences. Because phenomenology is systematic, it has characteristic actions and interventions – skills – and if these are not followed, the results may not be reliable.

Phenomenology acknowledges both the objective and the subjective and finds the relationship between them. It can be applied to many fields. Existential philosophy has benefited greatly from this method. Existential therapists have applied Husserl's ideas to the practice of therapy but phenomenology is equally important to psychological research.

Husserl's cornerstone is the principle of intentionality, the idea that we are always conscious of something. We are simultaneously conscious of the world, relating to the world and making meaning out of the world – we are never simply observers, we are always *participant* observers. A simple example of this is that one person's view of their relationship with someone will be different from the other person's view of the same relationship.

In following the rules of phenomenology:

- I form a clearer conception of how I relate to the world.
- I come to understand the world better.
- I understand the self which is created in the process of relating.

Literally, phenomenology means the study of events and things as they show themselves. This does not mean that the appearance of something is all there is, just that we should not assume anything about it. In being phenomenological, the existential therapist endeavours to put aside their assumptions about what the client is saying and aims just to listen and be curious about what it all means.

Husserl called our tendency to see the things we want to see, our natural way of seeing. He proposed a way to reduce the effect of this natural attitude and see things as if for the first time. We sometimes get a glimpse of this when we go on holiday to somewhere new and notice it with a more heightened sense of awareness than at home where we are surrounded by familiar objects. Children can do this more easily than adults – to them everything is new.

Becoming aware of our worldview allows us to understand that ours is only one vantage point among many. The more we become aware of our own personal map, the more we can put it aside and concentrate on the territory. The task of the existential therapist is to facilitate this process of discovery and appreciation of different standpoints.

Phenomenology asks: How can we understand anything without first understanding that which does the understanding?

EXERCISE

Take an everyday object, like a paper clip, a milk carton or a newspaper. Without assessing effectiveness or value, think of 20 other uses for the object. What did you have to do in order to stop thinking of the object in terms of its original use?

> ## KEY POINTS
>
> - We are always making sense of the world, we can never be free of our assumptions.
> - In order to get a more accurate picture of the world, we need to understand how we make sense of it.
> - By attending – just noticing, describing – not explaining, and not pre-judging, we can get a better idea of our assumptions.
> - Existential therapy is a phenomenological research project for both therapist and client.
> - Phenomenology allows us to comply with the rigorous standards of philosophical research and verification as well as those of human interaction and encounter.
> - It is the client's own narrative that leads the way, not the therapist's theoretical model or personal biases.

THE ASSUMPTIONS OF EXISTENTIAL THERAPY

It is impossible for any act to be free of assumptions and clients in existential therapy can only benefit if they go along with its basic assumptions which are:

- It is possible to make sense of life.
- It is good sense to do so.
- Each person has the capacity for making informed decisions about life and their attitude towards it.
- Difficult issues will not be resolved by being avoided.
- Human nature is basically flexible.
- People are able to learn from life and transcend problems.

Therefore, some clients may leave if they do not get on with these basic assumptions. They may want something more prescriptive or didactic. Existential therapy is not for everyone.

QUESTIONING ASSUMPTIONS

Questioning is at the heart of existential therapy but it is a collaborative 'questioning-with' rather than an interrogative 'questioning-of'. We are not lawyers, journalists or police officers. We are trying to find out something about the other person's life we do not already know. But most of all we question ourselves about the best way to tackle life problems.

But first of all we need to question our assumptions, judgements, biases and prejudices of how life and the world are or should be. The client's own concern and distress about their life, shown by their presence in therapy, indicate that their assumptions are flawed, erroneous, inconsistent or unexamined.

What is important is not whether or not they are objectively correct, but what they mean and how they inform the client's decisions about their life, and whether these choices are satisfactory. What matters most is the extent to which the client is able to take charge of life and accomplish their goals in life with awareness, courage and understanding.

Existentially, all assumptions relate to the givens of existence. These are:

- *Physical assumptions* like, 'My children will not die before me'.
- *Social assumptions* like, 'My intimate relationships are always of a particular quality'.
- *Psychological assumptions* like, 'I never get to do things the way I want'.
- *Spiritual/ethical assumptions* like, 'People will be punished if they do bad things'.

EXERCISE

Write about one of your assumptions on each of the four levels as indicated below for 15 minutes. Then read through it and think about what it was like writing it and what assumptions are embedded in it.

1 What I intend to do before I die.
2 How I get on with my friends.
3 What I owe myself in my life and what I do to get it.
4 My moral values and how I live up to them.

KEY POINTS

- Questioning is done in a spirit of curiosity, not in a spirit of criticism.
- We can become aware of our own bias and prejudice.
- In focussing on our own worldview, we make it both more visible and more transparent.

WORKING PHENOMENOLOGICALLY

Attention

Phenomenological practice begins with and is sustained by attention. Our ability to attend fully to our clients is the starting point of all good therapy. When encountering anything, we turn our attention to it. Immediately, we think about it in terms of what seems similar. We can't help it, it's what we do as meaning-creating creatures. It is the 'natural attitude'.

What we need to do instead is just to attend. It is important to train yourself to simply observe, listen and attend. Take time to notice and observe and describe and you will begin to get the hang of working phenomenologically.

Once we have begun to attend and describe properly, we can move on and there are then two further parts to the practice of phenomenology:

Epoché

In the first part through becoming aware of the object of our attention we become increasingly aware of our assumptions about it. This whole process is called *Epoché*, or literally the suspension of our judgements. As a result of our increasing awareness of our assumptions we are able to put them in metaphorical brackets so that we can see the object clearer. But we cannot do it just like that. We have to become aware of our assumptions first. It is also not enough just to know what they are, we also have to understand what they mean to us, and how they are a part of our way of habitually understanding the world. But also we have to understand that we can never be fully aware of them. This is a part of the principle of intentionality, that I can never be parted from my assumptions about the world but what I can do is to become as aware of them as possible. Although sometimes called a rule, it is better to think of it as an aim, since it can actually never be fully achieved. Though bracketing is an aspect of the *Epoché*, it generally only refers to the practical task of dealing with our assumptions by clearly separating them from our observations of the world. *Epoché* itself requires the entire sequence of awareness of world, suspension of judgement, description, awareness of assumptions, bracketing of assumptions, dealing with assumptions, returning to awareness.

Verification

The second part is called *verification*. This has a more hermeneutic function, which is to say that it is interpretive. In verification, we discipline ourselves to keep returning to the realities we are presented with and to check that our observations are correct and relate directly to the objects of our observations. We use our intuition and direct grasp of what is real to return to what is actually the case and what it is we are observing and describing. This allows us to start to understand the meanings of what has previously only been described. But each interpretation needs to be verified for its accordance with the truth. We compare what sense we make of the world with what is actual.

Becoming aware of assumptions

There are many things we have assumptions about. To begin with, we have assumptions in the process of looking, thinking and feeling. We might, for instance, think or feel about something with suspicion, curiosity or glee. This is what Husserl called the *Noesis,* the quality of the process of being aware. Then we also have assumptions about the object of our consciousness – what Husserl called the *Noema*. And finally we have assumptions about ourselves as we are conscious. Husserl called this thinking subject the cogito, or transcendental ego when divested of its assumptions. All of these are like filters that distorts how we see the world. The way we look at the world determines what we see in the world. Only when we have become aware enough of the way we habitually distort will we be in a position to respond in a way respectful of the client's autonomy and to reflect on the way they are restricting their freedom.

But every intervention the therapist makes, and this includes silence, expresses basic assumptions about life, the client and themselves and on many occasions this will not be particularly intrusive or damaging. We are not saying that assumptions are bad, rather that unexamined or unknown assumptions are likely to restrict the work. One danger of the therapist's unexamined assumptions is that the client will feel that the therapist's assumptions are facts which they will either agree with or react against. Not understanding what they mean to us is a denial and an evasion of our responsibility to ourselves and our clients.

We can never get away from our assumptions – this is a paradox because we need these assumptions, not just to make sense of the world but to remind ourselves how we usually make sense of the world. Our clients also need us to have these assumptions, but only if we know what to do with them. Our attempt at bracketing is the protection our clients have from our assumptions taking over and turning therapy into a sophisticated form of suggestion. Supervision is a good time for working out which assumptions need bracketing and how to work out and make sense of the bits of the equation in brackets.

Life is continuous, so reflecting on our evolving assumptions is continuous.

Before the session

Before seeing a client we need to prepare ourselves for the concentrated attention we will be giving. It is important to prepare yourself for your sessions. Arrive at the room you use some time before the start of the session, arrange the room, sit in the client's chair and imagine being the client to your therapist, move to your usual chair and compare the two experiences. Take note of the different views of the room – what the client can see that you cannot and vice versa. Acknowledge the time of day of the session because this makes a difference to the quality of attention you can offer.

Ask yourself questions like:

- Am I a morning or an evening sort of person? What difference does it make to me?
- What are my current preoccupations? What am I thinking of?
- What are my background feelings?

  o Am I tired? Why?
  o Am I excited? About what?
  o Am I worried? For what reason?

- Am I looking forward to the next few hours? Why?/why not?
- Am I composed and steady? How?

By doing this you begin the process of bringing your biases and blind spots into awareness. This will enable you to see, hear and relate more clearly.

During the session

All the above questions continue when the client comes into the room but they become more specific. We always have some overall emotional tone or colouring that influences how we see the world. We need to start with how we feel because this is the most obvious aspect of our existence.

We obviously need to concentrate on what is being said to us and on maintaining the relationship, but before we can make any sense of this we need to ask ourselves some further questions.

Bearing in mind how I am feeling today,

- what is it like to be with the client now, who is scared, resentful, seductive or angry with me?
- what is it like to never get eye contact/never avoid eye contact with the client?
- what is it like to sit in silence with this client/never get any silence with this client?

Asking these sort of background questions enables us to get a sense of the difference between ourselves and the client. It might be that a therapist habitually feels heavy and lethargic with one client but invigorated by another. These observations must be taken note of and wondered about either in supervision or in personal therapy.

On a skills level, we need to begin in silence and with full attention. The more we are freed up from having to talk, the more we can attend and hear. Our awareness is like a light we shine on things in order to understand them. This is not such a bad analogy because we know that if we shine a very bright light on something, it appears two-dimensional and throws no shadows. We need to throw just enough light in order to see, but not so much that we inhibit and flatten the experience, blinding our client. Bear in mind all the time that we are, despite our best efforts, always influencing the client. But by being phenomenological we might just find out about the nature of this influence.

Our ability to attend is correlated with our ability to live with uncertainty – the two alternatives being, on the one hand, muddle and vagueness, and, on the other, unthinking lazy dogmatism. If we find our attention wandering or searching for an explanation or a theory, it might mean that we are not attending well enough.

ILLUSTRATION

WHEN ASSUMPTIONS ABOUT FEELINGS WERE MISTAKEN

Paul came to short-term therapy because he was having relationships with two women, Jan and Lynn, who did not know of each other's existence and while he felt guilty, he was unable to leave either one. His therapist knew that she should put aside what she thought of the relationships and help Paul to make his own decision and she did this as well as she knew how. At the end of the therapy Paul thanked his therapist for listening and helping him tease out some of the issues to do with his inability to choose and commit. He said, 'I still don't know what to do, but I know who you think I should be with: Lynn.' His therapist was taken aback by this because it was in fact true that she preferred the sound of Lynn to Jan. Paul carried on, '… because you always paid a bit more attention to my misgivings about Jan than you did with those of Lynn. But at least you didn't tell me what to do.'

(Continued)

(Continued)

Commentary

It is impossible to put aside, to bracket our opinions completely. Paul felt that the quality of attention he got from his therapist was what he needed to explore his issue in the time available. Although he was aware of his therapist's feelings, he did not find they prevented him from exploring his issue. Not being able to put aside her feelings about Jan, the therapist did not notice she had expressed a personal preference.

How do you spot your own biases and assumptions?

A good start is five simple questions you can ask yourself about your work with particular clients:

1 What do I want for my client?
2 If I were to give my client some advice right now, what might it be?
3 Do I feel differently towards this client rather than towards other clients? And what is this about?
4 Was my request for information just to satisfy my own curiosity?
5 Why did I make that self-disclosure?

ILLUSTRATION

WHEN ASSUMPTIONS ABOUT CONTENT WERE MISTAKEN

Maria was referred by her GP because of difficulties she was having at work and getting on with her family. At the first session she described her issues and said that she was sometimes a bit 'cheesed off' by it all but that she had bought a book about depression and was working her way through it. She seemed quite upbeat in this first session so the counsellor decided that there was no more need for sessions and Maria agreed. The next thing the counsellor knew was a note from the GP asking why Maria had been signed off as she was suicidal.

Commentary

The counsellor's first mistake was assuming that Maria's meaning of the phrase 'cheesed off' was the same as his own, which was as a very mild term describing a temporary state. The second was taking the reference to the self-help book literally and not seeing it as possibly also meaning that there was no point going on with counselling. He did not pick up on the gravity of Maria's situation because he did not query the meaning.

The answers to these five simple questions will enable you to become aware of your assumptions about both content and process. We all want to think of ourselves as good ethical practitioners and often our first answers will reflect this. But we need to develop a way of questioning our own answers. Of not accepting the first answer we give ourselves.

Description

Another way we can help our assumptions to come to light is by trying to describe and not explain by attributing causation, problem solving or analysing. At first glance, this looks easy but it is not.

Therapists and counsellors are used to explaining their work to other professionals and it is hard to get out of the habit, but in therapy explanation is both unnecessary and distancing. Everything the therapist says needs to be as close to the client's experience as possible, what we call 'experience-near', and needs to try to make the client's engagement with their experience closer. Theory tends to be distancing, therefore theoretical concepts, including philosophical ones, have little place in the consulting room.

As a general rule, the temptation for the therapist to explain is proportional to their anxiety – to how much discomfort the therapist is feeling about being with the client. In other words, explanation is invariably given to relieve the therapist's confusion, not the client's. Consequently it usually increases the client's confusion.

EXERCISE

Take an everyday object, like a chair, move it to the middle of a room and look at it for 5 minutes as if you've never seen it before. Describe what you see. Do not describe it in terms of 'chairness' or attempt to explain why it is as it is or what any of the parts are there for. If you find it difficult, turn it upside down and try again. At the end, reflect on what it was like to 'see' the chair as you never 'saw' it before.

The most useful question to start a descriptive analysis is not 'Why?', because this distances from present experience and is only answerable with 'because ...' , which prompts yet another 'Why?' question, but the questions 'What?' and 'How?', which simply request further description.

In terms of specific verbal interventions this philosophical principle can be translated into the following questions:

- How do you mean?
- What's that like?

- Can you give me an example?
- Can you say a bit more about that?

These simple requests can easily be translated into one's own personal language, with the important qualification that the spirit of description, not explanation, be adhered to.

Closed and suggestive questions like: 'Have you thought of getting another job?', or 'Are you going to get a divorce?', not only close down the emerging dialogue but say more about the therapist's unexamined assumptions than about the client's investigation.

At the beginning of the work, therapists need to restrict themselves to what the client has said and concentrate on the various emotions, concepts and actions referred to, while gathering more information. As a general rule, the further away from the present moment you go at the start of the work, into the past or the future, the greater the risk there is that you will hi-jack the conversation and start talking about what you as the therapist want to talk about. As time goes on, when the therapist and client have built up a rapport, risks can be taken and links can be made. Therefore the use of therapist metaphors in the early part of therapy is not advised because of the likelihood that the therapist will inhibit the client's emerging ability to describe her experience in her own terms.

While it is important to stay with the client's own words, we cannot assume that:

- what a client says is a complete, accurate or literal description of their experience;
- if a client says 'yes' they agree with us or think the same way as us;
- the client knows what words to use;
- the client wants to tell you about their experience even if they are able;
- the experience is either currently or eventually verbalizable.

Lets explore this a little bit further. To hold to any of these assumptions restricts our openness. But to concentrate only on what is spoken is to put too great an emphasis on the reliability of language. It can be argued that verbal cues are only obvious to us because we live in a verbal culture and psychotherapy is a symptom of this culture.

We are much more than just the words we use.

Equalization

Another source of assumptions is regarding what we think is important in what the client is saying. On many occasions in therapy the client knows no more than they are telling us. And neither of us knows what any of it means.

In equalizing, we need to consider each part of the content, the process and the experience of the client as of equal importance. Our ability to listen will always be distorted by our own life experience and our ability to convince ourselves of a particular way of seeing is enormous. Therefore our success is dependent on our ability to notice and deal with our assumptions. These will often be due to identifying with the client too much and forgetting that their life is different to ours. We are mistakenly seeing the client out of their context. Or to put it another way, if we catch ourselves thinking about our clients in particular ways, it gives a clue that we are not equalizing well enough.

ILLUSTRATION

NARROWLY AVOIDING THE CONSEQUENCES OF NOT EQUALIZING

As a therapist, Nick prided himself on his non-reliance on technology. He asked his clients to switch their phones off in the session. His client Sandra often forgot and these sessions were interrupted by Sandra's phone ringing. On the twelfth session she came five minutes late and spent the next few minutes working on her phone. Nick was just about to comment on the malign influence of mobile phones in general and in the therapy relationship in particular when Sandra said, 'I've been making some notes on my phone about last week's session and my thoughts in the week and I'm just reminding myself because I want to make the best use of this time.' Nick was taken aback because he did not even know that phones could be used for such things.

Commentary

Nick had an assumption that mobile phones were not useful additions to life. He had also decided that Sandra's use of her phone was not helping her. These assumptions were so firmly held that they were not questioned. Alternatives could not be entertained. By Sandra explaining what she was doing, Nick was able to realize that he was wrong and narrowly avoided showing his assumptions and his misplaced anger in such a way that could have risked the therapeutic relationship.

We should also be asking ourselves things like:

- In what way am I influencing my clients so they never talk about sex, or envy, or death, which I also happen to not like talking about, or they always talk about creativity or wholeness, which I do like talking about?

However, as long as one is describing the elements of the narrative if only to oneself, sooner or later certain elements will begin to stand out.

ILLUSTRATION

USING BASIC PHENOMENOLOGICAL INTERVENTIONS TO OPEN OUT A DIALOGUE

Session 14

Don:	It hasn't been very good this week.
Therapist:	Hmm?
Don:	Work has been difficult.
Therapist:	In what way?
Don:	It's the manager again.
Therapist:	How do you mean?
Don:	Oh, the usual things.
Therapist:	Can you give me an example?
Don:	He asked me and my colleague to do the same report.
Therapist:	What was that like for you?
Don:	Really annoying.
Therapist:	Can you say a bit more?
Don:	and humiliating because I feel my colleague is better than me at that job.
Therapist:	Hmm?
Don:	I feel it's a sort of test, I want to do well but I feel he's trying to catch me out.
Therapist:	What's that like?

(continued below)

Commentary

By simple requests for description and detail the dialogue was opened out and the client's engagement with the issue made deeper. The client's natural curiosity about himself was encouraged by attention, description and equalization.

Horizontalization

The skills of the first stage, of *Epoché*, are mainly clarificatory, and those of the next stage of *verification* are interpretive. The bridge between the two is *horizontalizing*, when we endeavour to place what is becoming known against a horizon, to contextualize the client's worldview. This is crucial to prevent the work becoming purely introspective. The client's view clearly needs to be taken seriously but we need to remember that it is always placed within a context and that the context is often ignored, evaded or denied. Simply to place the experience back into its context can have the effect of providing the client with a new perspective on their own life. This in itself can sometimes feel like a great relief: it is as if the client suddenly sees him or herself from an objective perspective and can have understanding for their predicament rather than feeling trapped in it from the inside. Our world is always situated in a context. It can help enormously to describe our situation and place in the world, in order to re-establish some perspective. The client's readiness to move from work that is primarily about clarification, to work that can include verification will be indicated by their realization that their conclusions, thoughts and feelings are context contingent personal responses rather than being derived from causation or fact. Any attempt to verify prior to this will be premature and probably lead to an intellectualized dialogue or to the therapist leading the client.

Verification and interpretation

Attention and requests for further description and perspective can be extremely powerful and on some occasions can rekindle genuine philosophical perplexity and personal questioning, but on most occasions it is not enough. This can lead to a morbid going round in circles when almost literally, nothing happens. You are both busy finding out things you already know. Our clients deserve something better and we both have better things to do with our time. Verification in a manner that is sensitive to the client's being is almost a definition of effective therapy. It is a way of joining with the client and extending their sense of who they are in the depth of their being. It gives a person a feeling that what they experience matters and is taken seriously and can be understood and perhaps even altered or overcome.

In verification we are able to do something with all the impressions and questions accumulated during *Epoché*. It is where we break the principle of equalization and it is necessary for the therapy to progress. But we have to make sure that when we do it, it is because the client has told us that one part of their life is more important than another, and not just because we think it is. It is also in verification that we can bring to light the way the client is struggling with the givens of existence, such as temporality, paradox, dilemma and evasion of responsibility.

The overall aim of verification in therapy is to explore meanings, both within the content, the process, and the relationship between the therapist and the client and to make links between them. It is about wondering about how all the elements are related. We are wondering what similarities there are, and how the jigsaw fits together, for fit together it must. We are therefore looking for common elements in the content and process to wonder about and draw conclusions from.

There are three dangers here:

- The common elements must belong together by virtue of themselves, and not by virtue of the therapist's unexamined assumptions or desire for cleverness or closure.
- It is extremely difficult to judge at what point enough evidence has been gathered to justify breaking the rule of equalization and to select a particular item to focus on. This is something that has to be learnt through trial and error and applied with continuous monitoring.

- Not acknowledging that some elements are more in evidence than others is doing a disservice to yourself and your clients. A reluctance to rely on the authority of your own experience can lead to an idealization of ignorance. This is sometimes referred to as unknowing, but can easily turn into a determination not to know. Hiding behind ignorance can lead to nihilism and insecurity in the client and can be as damaging as hiding behind theory.

Two rules to go by are:

1 If the same issue has been mentioned several times, it is usually worth picking out and referring to directly for further exploration. You may not hear it again if you do not, for the client may give up mentioning it, presuming you are not interested in their concern.
2 If something clearly has unacknowledged emotional tone attached to it, it may be worth picking out for further examination and probing, especially by referring to the state of mind it is related to.

Characteristic statements or intentions of verification are:

- **'What is your part in what you are describing?'** This brings present responsibility into the dialogue and questions the client's denial of responsibility and their sense of separation from both their own life and the lives of others.
- **'Has this ever happened before in your life? Is this feeling familiar?'** This introduces the past, previous experience, into the dialogue and looks to finding the universals behind the individual properties.
- **'How is this leading you to what you say you want?'** This introduces the future, hope, and change, into the dialogue. It reconnects the client with their life project.
- **'On the one hand you feel ... but on the other hand you feel ....'** This draws the client's attention to the dilemmas, contradictions and the tension between opposites that they usually try to avoid. It highlights the dynamic nature of emotional life and helps them to face up to their inner and outer reality, gaining strength from their ability to do so. Often this leads to the discovery of a paradox.

Verification is similar to interpretation and existentially we are always interpreting because we are always making sense of reality. All therapy is interpretive in the sense that issues are considered and meanings and possibilities discerned: new connections are made and new meanings are discovered all the time. This means that all our interventions are interpretive; some are just more complex than others. In a narrower and more formal sense, an interpretation is a way of compressing an enormous amount of information into a few words, in order to capture, organize and understand it in a new way. This has two functions. One is to bring things out in the open in a way that allows the client to take notice of their experience, get a hold of it and grasp it. The other is to help them consolidate the work being done and to make clear and clean connections between new and old insights, so that their worldview becomes ever more coherent and consistent with reality. Above all, such interpretations must fit with the client's own evolving understanding of the world and enhance meaning and deepen engagement with the issues at hand. Interpretations should never impose the therapist's worldview or theoretical dogma, nor should they oversimplify the client's experience, nor distance the client from it, for instance, by having a tone of infantilization or intellectualization. In the ebb and flow of the interaction the therapist needs to cultivate a spirit of creative uncertainty. Therefore silence itself can have a powerful interpretive value, since it can request the client to think about the meanings that are being traced and stay with their sensations, feelings, thoughts and intuitions. Interpretations should be kept as short and simple as possible, as long interpretations can be confusing and also hinder the development of the client's self-reflective capacity.

There are four qualities that a successful interpretation must have:

1 **Simplicity:** The interpretation must be tentative but also crystal clear for the client to be able to consider it, rather than feel obligated to swallow it whole and agree with it or reject it without considering it. However, there is a danger here since too much tentativeness can be confusing and the client may be unclear about what we are saying. The ideal is an approach which goes from one bit of meaning to the next, step by step, until things make sense and fall into place. It is part of an enquiry into the client's truth. The therapist can state emerging meanings firmly, while encouraging the client to verify, correct and refine until it fits just right. Typically this means that the client is the one who formulates the final definition of their experience. The therapist may elicit this by saying things like: 'what I just said did not sit quite right with you' or 'that isn't exactly it yet, is it?'

2 **Connectivity:** Any interpretations we make must have a direct connection between a trigger event that the client is currently preoccupied with and the internal and external consequences it has in the client's life. Ideally it connects something we already know about how the client is, with a new understanding of it, while highlighting the client's active part in it. Therefore the focus has to be on linking a present experience with the past and/or and future-as-currently-lived, rather than on the past-as-it-was, or the future-as-it may be. The aim is to reinforce a sense of ownership and authorship for the client and to ensure that they take pleasure in their ability to trace the truths of their life and make alterations in their own life that improve their sense of living for real.

3 **Coherence:** The duty of a therapist is to make sure that interpretations are made within the client's framework rather than within their own theory or that of their supervisor. This obviously means that the therapist is clearing their own bias and their own assumptions as much as possible at all times and is willing to enter into a process of debate and discussion whenever a client disagrees with their words or their perceptions of the client's life. Such disagreements are often the sine qua non of true progress. The angle from which the therapist approaches the client's life may be biased but it is nevertheless a focused view that can serve to help the client get their own focus into sharper detail while gaining a wider perspective at the same time because of the therapist's view from elsewhere. As long as the therapist is willing to engage fully in this process and to gather connections and meanings in order to be questioned and contradicted, teaching the client the pleasure of probing and facing up, the process will remain alive, and vital new understandings will be gathered. Such work invariably teaches the therapist as much as the client, is challenging, engaging and though often demanding, usually pleasurable and productive for both.

4 **Relevance:** Timing the interpretive intervention is crucial and the therapist will use a combination of their attunement to the client and their knowledge of the client to place their interpretations. Thinking of interpretations as discrete statements is to miss their point. Interpretations made too early or too late are either irrelevant or distracting and those said at the same time as the client has the insight are unnecessary. It is the work as a whole which is interpretive, or rather hermeneutic, in that therapy is a joint search for meaning. A 'wrong' interpretation at the right time will be as counterproductive, if not more, than the 'correct' interpretation at the wrong time.

Therefore the emphasis is ultimately always on the authority of the client. We model clarity and openness so that the client can learn to articulate their own living experience for themselves with increasing authority. All the meanings that are agreed in therapy must be compatible with the client's own understanding of the world and consistent with a growing capacity of owning their lives as well as with their building confidence in their ability to understand and articulate and make sense of their experience.

ILLUSTRATION

USING BASIC AND VERIFICATION INTERVENTIONS TO OPEN OUT AND DEEPEN A DIALOGUE

(Continued from above)

Don:	I feel it's a sort of test, I want to do well but I feel he's trying to catch me out.
Therapist:	What's that like?
Don:	I can't stand it. It's always the same.
Therapist:	'Always the same', you mean it's happened before?
Don:	Well, yes, it's the story of my life. Everyone does this to me.
Therapist:	'Everyone'?
Don:	My parents, my partner, they all do it.
Therapist:	Do you?
Don:	Do I what?
Therapist:	I wondered to what extent *you* catch yourself out.
Don:	What do you mean?
Therapist:	You say on the one hand that you want to show your competence but on the other hand you back down when there's competition.
Don:	I don't understand.
Therapist:	I wondered what you get out of making yourself second best, perhaps it's safer in some way?
Don:	I don't know, it's certainly familiar.
Therapist:	'Familiar'?
Don:	I know where I am with it, it's sort of comfortable.
Therapist:	It's comfortable?
Don:	Well, yes, more comfortable than succeeding, in a funny sort of way.

Therapist:	Can you say a bit more?
Don:	I think I'm a bit afraid of success.
Therapist:	How do you mean?
Don:	I'd feel exposed and have to show myself, which is silly because I know I can, but ...
Therapist:	But?
Don:	I don't know.
Therapist:	But you'd have to change the way you think about yourself as successful rather than unsuccessful?
Don:	Yes, I suppose so.

(Continued below)

Commentary

By a combination of bracketing and verification interventions the dialogue was opened out and became much more personal so that Don was able to consider the part he played in the circumstances that he previously considered only to happen to him.

Getting a wider perspective on life

The result of becoming attuned to the emotional tone that affects the way in which I see the world, is that I get to understand myself. As I become more aware of the restricted way I understand events, I get to see myself as not just at the centre of my world but also as one person among many. It becomes more obvious that 'I' am a part of an interconnected 'we', all subject to the same givens and mystery of existence. An implication of this is that although a client may wish to find out why things happened as they did, the likelihood is that they never will. This not only brings humility and acceptance but illuminates a basic paradox of life that my intentionality generates me at the same time as it seems to be generated by me. In horizontalizing our interventions, we seek to explore the context of a person's experience. We broaden out their understanding of their world by extending their perspective and touching the wider horizon of their life.

ILLUSTRATION

(Continued from above some sessions later)

Don:	You know, I've been blaming others for years, like that person at work, for things that I can't do.
Therapist:	Yes?
Don:	And that's wrong, isn't it? It doesn't make sense, it can't all be his fault, can it, it can only be mine.

(Continued)

(Continued)

Therapist: How do you mean?

Don: I've been making him responsible for how I feel, making out it's his problem, well, it might be, I don't know, but what I do know is that it's mine.

Therapist: Where does that lead you?

Don: Well, I'm beginning to realize what I was doing all that time, no wonder people used to get fed up with me.

Therapist: How does that feel?

Don: A lot of things, foolish, embarrassed, guilty, but also humble. But you know what, it's weird because I think I understand them more now that I understand myself more. Before, I thought I did but I didn't at all. I was imagining it all. I'm just like other people and that's great, I used to think it was bad but it's not, is it?

Therapist: What's that like to come to this now?

Don: It's scary, but liberating.

Therapist: How so?

Don: Well, I know that I have a point of view but also that others have theirs but where that used to be intimidating and depressing, it's now exciting. There's no other choice, is there? I can't decide exactly how other people are going to think can I, but …

Therapist: But what?

Don: But it's up to me, I can make my own life and not wait for it to be given to me or taken away. I can only do it with them and they with me, from here.

Commentary

By a combination of basic and advanced phenomenological interventions Don is able not just to see that some of the things he does are counterproductive and to take ownership of these but also to see himself in the wider context of humanity.

KEY POINTS

- By becoming aware of our assumptions and bracketing them we can cultivate a spirit of active curiosity.
- The intention is always to open out possibility, not to close it down.
- The clarity which comes from an understanding of the complexity and richness of experience is enhanced by description, not by explanation.
- The client's autonomy is respected at all times.
- The client is enabled to combine a subjective and an objective view on their own life in order to get an accurate sense of horizon and depth.
- We need to constantly monitor our emotional responses to our clients and take them seriously but not necessarily literally. They are valuable insights into the evolving therapeutic relationship and can be examined in depth in supervision of personal therapy.

4

DEVELOPING
AN EXISTENTIAL
ATTITUDE

> He who has a why to live for can bear almost any how.
>
> Friedrich Nietzsche

OPENNESS TO EXPERIENCE

As we have seen, existentially the sense of self is fluid rather than fixed, being continuously co-created by the person's interactions in the world. In this way the worldview is constructed. But because it is so personal, we expect others to perceive the world in the same way and we are constantly reminded that they do not.

Their view always reveals a new perspective that offers us the possibility of altering our own view and getting a bit closer to truth, if we are open to it. This is phenomenology in everyday life.

However, we selectively interact with the world so that it conforms to our standards and expectations. We unwittingly repeat our past mistakes, often excusing them with comments like, 'I don't know why, it's just the way I am.'

Existential therapists refer to this as 'sedimentation': it is as if the sediments of the river of life fall to the river floor and give us an increasingly solid but illusory sense of identity that dams up our life. Much of the time we prefer past certainties over future possibilities. But when the blockage is broken, the flow can get re-established and life can resume its full flow and necessarily unpredictable course. But this is rarely easy because there is always a tension between the wish to be solid and fixed and the awareness that we are not.

We all have limitations as to how open we can be to chance and opportunity in daily life. Some of us welcome it; others do not. The restriction and distortion of our capacity to be open translate into our physical space and lead to the conditions known as claustrophobia or agoraphobia. In this, it is as if the space itself, as well as the presence or absence of other people in it, has a threatening quality that leads to restriction of our personal will and of our capacity to exercise freedom and choice. In claustrophobia, we feel hemmed in and suffocated. In agoraphobia, we feel exposed and unprotected.

Clients come to see us when they feel out of touch with the natural flow of their lives. Earlier ways of doing things are no longer useful and are likely to be experienced more as restrictions or threats. They may describe such experiences as anxiety, depression, confusion or stress. Much of therapy is about helping another person to return to a position of openness to themselves, to the world, to others and to life itself.

That we feel anxiety at all is evidence of the tension between the necessity to be open and the fear of what may happen if we are. But often we are out of touch with the gains we can make by being open rather than closed. And sometimes we are so open that we feel overwhelmed.

Anxiety is based on the fundamental ontological anxiety of being alive and there are two principal ways of protecting ourselves from this ontological insecurity. One is by pretending that we are free in a world of facts and can be summarized as 'I can do anything I like.' This is sometimes called a manic defence. Others may refer to it as self-confidence or 'attitude'. For people with too much of this sort of confidence, exposure to the reality of vulnerability and limitations will be problematic. For those with too little, it will be necessary to risk taking a chance on oneself and finding that the world can respond differently.

ILLUSTRATION
BEING FREE IN A WORLD OF FACTS

Adam came to counselling because he needed to 'get a bit of perspective on his life and plan a bit'. He had recently lost his job, and his girl-friend had walked out on him leaving him with large debts. Initially his counsellor was impressed by his resilience and ability to carry on and to look on the bright side and think of alternatives but as time went on she noticed he was curiously unaffected by events, almost as if he was totally out of touch. He was unwilling to explore his part in his life. 'I can't see the point ... I want to think about the future.' Although he was polite, she felt disregarded. Although they had contracted for 12 sessions he came to the fourth session saying it would be the last. He had decided what to do. He was going to get a bank loan to go travelling for a year or more and had simply come to say thank you and goodbye.

Commentary

Adam needed to see himself as separate from other people so that he would not be affected by them. This was reflected in the therapeutic relationship, where he could not really allow the therapist to be in relation with him. His need to see himself as invulnerable led him to disregard not just other people in his life but himself too and also the likely consequences of his actions. He thought he could start all over again simply by ignoring present reality and that he did not need to learn the lessons of the past. It was not surprising then that this strategy turned out not to be successful.

The second way is to pretend to be a fact in a world of freedom and it can be summarized as 'I can't do anything I like.' It is sometimes called learnt helplessness or depression. We make ourselves into rigidly defined entities and dismiss the possibility of change by rejecting the freedom to choose how to respond.

ILLUSTRATION

BEING A FACT IN A WORLD OF FREEDOM

Beth came to counselling because she was 'depressed'. She left university three years before where she did a subject she was competent at but not greatly interested in. She said: 'Everyone thought I ought to do it so I did.' Since then she had had a succession of temporary jobs. The last one of these, in sales, she wanted to continue in but her employers said that she needed to be more outgoing. This upset her. She said: 'I know I've got to be but I don't know how. I'm scared by all the other very bubbly people there ... and also by the customers. I thought it might make me different, bring me out of myself, but it's done the opposite.' A friend said she should try counselling because it would give her new tools she could use. She said: 'I know what I should do but don't get round to it ... I feel the world is leaving me behind.' She tended to talk about 'everyone thinks that ...' and 'other people can do ...'. Although she was keen for the counsellor to tell her what to do, she met even simple requests for clarification or concrete examples with a look of bafflement which often led to her saying, 'Oh, I don't know ... I can't think ... I'm no good at this.'

Commentary

Beth had either not had sufficient experience of making and acting on her own choices or not been able to make use of the experience she had had. Consequently she saw herself as someone who could not act autonomously. She could not tolerate the anxiety of the result of her choice, whether it was a success or failure. She tried to avoid the anxiety by avoiding the choice not realizing that the avoidance was itself a choice and blocked her life. Although intellectually intelligent she appeared to prefer the apparent safety of thinking of herself as acted on by others and valuing other people's opinions over her own. Because of her anxiety at taking responsibility for her choices, she gave responsibility for herself to others. Only when realizing how she did this could things begin to ease up for her.

Neither the person who says: 'I can do anything I like', nor the person who says: 'I can't do anything I like', are true to existence. The reality of existence is that we have to be prepared to do what we can and that sometimes we succeed and sometimes we do not. But in exploring our abilities, we expand and practise them, becoming more able and more flexible in the process. If we are too audacious we may falter and fail and eventually may give up. If, on the contrary, we are too cowardly and avoid all risk and challenge, we may become paralysed by fear, lose flexibility and become weakened through lack of practice.

Existential therapists make it clear from the outset that they expect the client to have a basic commitment to be willing to examine whatever arises and confront its implications. Existential therapists will also know that trust has to be earned.

Clients for their part are entitled to expect that their therapist will also be open and will listen with sensitivity to the negative emotions such confessions invariably involve. Precisely because of this, the therapist will spend more time listening and understanding than talking and interpreting.

The existential therapist's primary concern is to maintain a balance between an attitude which invites openness without leading to a sense of abandonment, on the one hand, and which is attentive without being intrusive, on the other. The specific qualities and interventions used to promote this are dependent on the needs of the individual client in that moment and the personal qualities of the therapist and of the interaction they have established.

Once this fundamental listening and hearing process is established, it will be possible to explore more deeply, and this will often involve more challenging interventions which evoke conflicts in the client and also sometimes between client and therapist.

In fact, openness to experience involves conflict and our success at living is about meeting and resolving this conflict rather than avoiding it. The therapist has to model this willingness to face conflict and difficulty with equanimity.

Openness to silence

Judging the amount of silence a client needs at any moment is vital. Enough silence is sufficient silence to allow the client to pause for thought and be in the moment, and not so much that she drowns in it or becomes paralysed and overly self-conscious. It is never easy to find the right balance of silence and talk.

Existential therapists will pay attention to the ways clients are with others and with themselves, from what they say, how they place their chair, their body in the chair, their legs in the space between the chairs and the way in which they take up space in the dialogue. Some clients are reluctant to fill the space while some are reluctant to let the therapist contribute.

KEY POINTS

- By being phenomenological, we can become more aware of the way we interpret the world in narrow and often unrealistic ways.
- Listening with the right sort of openness and attentiveness is the foundation of all good practice.
- The task of existential therapy is one of facilitating the client to become freer to choose when to be open and when not to be open.
- Openness to experience means to be able to embrace autonomy and this is as true for the therapist as for the client.

BOUNDARIES AND CONSISTENCY

Research and personal experience tell us conclusively that people thrive when they are treated in a respectful and consistent manner and when the boundaries of the relationship are clear and sensitively adhered to. The therapeutic relationship is no different. It is just a specialized type of personal intimate relationship and in order for existential therapy to work, both client and therapist need to know where they stand and what they can reasonably expect from each other. On the whole, what works best is clarity combined with firm though somewhat flexible boundaries. The client thrives on a feeling that the therapist relates to her with sensitivity and attentiveness, yet without suffocating her with care. There is a real art to knowing how to precisely keep the therapeutic space open yet safely delimited.

Clients in existential therapy discover that through consistency, the relationship with the therapist can be experienced as freeing rather than restricting or abandoning. This freedom allows learning not only the rewards of intimacy but also crucially to explore its limits: they learn what they cannot get from others and what they need to get from themselves, and that although interpersonal encounter may temper existential isolation, it can never eliminate it. A flexible and responsive boundary does not move unpredictably and is always open for discussion.

Care is a common word in therapy and everyday life. It has implications of concern or liking, and in an explicit helping setting it has implications of 'taking care of' as in protection. The existential therapist understands the word 'care' in a particular sense. What is taken care of is the client's autonomy, and this is done by respecting and believing in the client's ability to make their own decisions about their life. This can sometimes be interpreted as harsh or uncaring, but it is actually based in reality and truth. One way in which existential therapists express their care is by being resilient, consistent and firm with boundaries. This is done by acknowledging problems, conflicts, issues and dilemmas, rather than denying or ignoring them. We need to demonstrate that we can live with them and are ready to be responsive and steady in the face of difficulties.

The principle of respect and consistency also applies to the management of the session. It means that therapists need to be reliable. We live busy lives and it is an element of everyday Western practice that most of our available working time is spoken for and time-tabled. If we say we will meet a client at 2 pm for 50 minutes, this means just that: that we will do everything we can to be there at 2pm and end the session at 2.50pm. We give them no more and no less than we have contracted and are present for them during this time, whether or not the client is on time. We do not hold grudges for lateness or cancelled sessions, since the client will pay for their time and can dispose of it as they wish. We also have a responsibility to help them become more aware of what choices lead them to be late or cancel.

ILLUSTRATION

HOLDING AND MAINTAINING BOUNDARIES

Danny first got in touch with his therapist by email in which he asked how the therapist worked and what her main theoretical influences were. The therapist focussed on the compatibility of their diaries instead. From experience she had found that the first thing to establish was whether her availability coincided with

(Continued)

(Continued)

her client. It did but Danny returned to his original questions. The therapist replied that the conversation should be continued in person in the first session. Danny agreed. He arrived a little late and talked immediately about his issue which was not being able to trust his partner. Towards the end of the session and after they had finished the contractual details which resulted in her agreeing to a slightly lower fee than usual, he said he had come out without any money. The therapist said that she would accept the money next week, same day, same time. Two days later she got an email from him with some more questions. She replied very briefly saying that she wished to keep the work within the appointment times and would talk with him at the next session. The work continued on in this vein with Danny pushing at the time, content and payment boundaries and the therapist having to stand firm, once saying that unless he paid, she would consider the sessions suspended. Gradually he acknowledged that although initially frustrating, he always knew where he was with the therapist and learnt to use the therapeutic space.

Commentary

The therapist knew that although superficially appealing, little would be achieved by answering Danny's questions. There would always be another question and the net effect would be to prevent Danny looking at his issue. It would be an evasion. At the same time she knew that ignoring it completely would not do. Not trusting his partner was reflected in not trusting her. She knew she had to address it and risk Danny's disapproval for the sake of the therapy. Indeed, Danny's disapproval and distrust became an issue which he fruitfully examined for the first time in therapy and he was able to appreciate the reliability of the space and his responsibility for it. This was only possible to happen after the therapist proved herself to be consistent and reliable.

Some existential therapists will begin a session by welcoming the client into the room, others by a hand-shake, others will do so with a summary hello. What is important is that every session will begin in a similar way, introducing an element of consistency. This will allow a clear and clean framework, within which variations will become obvious and meaningful, and therefore any disagreements or conflicts arising can be addressed and be understood. As said above, a flexible and responsive boundary does not move unpredictably but it is always up for discussion.

Although no particular techniques or interventions are prescribed, any intervention must be consistent with the principles of phenomenology in that they acknowledge the client's fundamental autonomy. The specific context of each therapeutic relationship combined with the appropriate professional and ethical demands will define the principles and boundaries to which the existential therapist will be consistent.

Everything we do has a reference to and a resonance with one or other of the givens of existence. In the case of boundaries, the physical boundaries of our lives are birth and death. They define our lives and the tensions they create can be creative, not destructive. In a similar way, we should be aware of the boundaries of care. It is sometimes easy to take responsibility for the client in such a way that the client's autonomy does not flourish. Many of the breaches of ethics acted on by professional organizations are about occasions when the client's autonomy is undermined.

KEY POINTS

- When we 'care about' someone, what we 'care for' is their autonomy.
- Consistent and clear boundaries lead to trust.
- Living a meaningful life means to acknowledge and live within the boundaries of existence.

MUTUALITY AND DIALOGUE

One of the great puzzles of human existence is to work out what other people are there for and how to get on with them. In philosophy this is called the problem of other minds. Each of us enters existence alone and must depart from it alone. And yet we are always surrounded by others, one way or another. What this means existentially is that no matter how close each of us becomes to another, there remains a final unbridgeable gap. There is always a tension between the awareness of our autonomy and our belonging with others.

The human being's universal conflict is therefore that while we strive to be individuals who set ourselves apart from others, we feel compelled to overcome this separation by relationships with others. This can sometimes lead to merging which in turn becomes threatening. There is no enduring solution to isolation. We have no alternative but to find a way to take it into ourselves and come to terms with it.

That mutuality is difficult is shown by the frequency with which people enter therapy because of relationship difficulties. People fear abandonment and harassment in equal measure. They try to solve the paradox either by fusion i.e. merging with another or by fission, i.e. separation from another. Neither of these is ultimately viable. If people can be helped to tolerate the inherent paradox in relationship they soon discover the freedom that intimacy can offer. This both–and solution can be summarized as: 'I have the responsibility to do what I want in a world of others, but so does everybody else and it works best if we take each other into account.'

Central to existential therapy is dialogue. Dialogue does not simply refer to what the therapist and client talk about. Both the nature and quality of the dialogue define the effectiveness of the therapy. We need to distinguish between monologue, duologue and dialogue.

Monologue

A monologue takes place when one person is talking and another is listening and the talker's main concern is to talk and has little concern about how he or she is received.

The listener's experience is often one of being talked at rather than being talked to or with. They do not feel included in the conversation.

Duologue

A duologue is when two people are talking to each other and only superficially listening to each other. They may well take it in turns to talk and to listen and even to respond to what each other says but they are not really hearing the other. They are more likely to be listening to what they want the other to say and can then respond to. Another way to think of this is as two simultaneous monologues.

Dialogue

A dialogue, on the other hand, is when the two people genuinely attend and listen to each other, not for what they want to hear the other say, but for what is actually being said and often also to what is being only hinted at. It involves a dual openness to the other and also to oneself. A true dialogue will always be characterized by a certain amount of anxiety which may be felt as excitement, but it is anxiety in the sense that one never knows what will happen. A true dialogue is dynamic. Anxiety is a quality of a live present relationship. In the therapeutic relationship both the therapist and the client should be feeling apprehensive about what will happen. If one or the other is not, then a dialogue will not be possible and there will be a duologue pretending to be a dialogue. They will be finding out things they already know. One can only discover something new if one is open and ready for the possibility of finding a new outlook on the world.

Although dialogue is usually thought of in terms of talking, it is primarily about listening and searching for meaning. The development of dialogue is down to the therapist evaluating how to provide and maintain an optimum amount of challenge and support. Most often this means the therapist is silent, at least at the start of therapy, but it is not always so. If the client needs the therapist just to listen, it is a mistake to talk and if the client needs the therapist to talk, it is a mistake to be silent. The route from monologue or duologue to dialogue will be different for each therapeutic relationship. But ultimately successful therapies end with dialogue.

ILLUSTRATION

THE EVOLUTION OF MONOLOGUE TO DIALOGUE

Peter began therapy with a great deal to talk about, his upbringing, his relationship with his brother and his parents, his recent relationship break-up, his unsatisfactory career choice and his unstable housing situation. He prepared what to say in each session and he had no shortage of things to say and his therapist found that not only did she not need to say anything, since he never asked her any questions, but also that anything she did say was usually interrupted after a few words as he would carry on as if she had not spoken. She felt battered and did not look forward to their sessions. She bracketed her own irritation and realized after a short while that there was a meaning in the process of this monologue, since he simply needed to be listened to. This she did. After a while through a combination of patience and attunement to his need for being attended to, she was able to point the dynamic out, simply as something that she understood about him and not as a criticism. This enabled him to listen to her, to someone else, and eventually to be comfortable enough in her company to be silent and open to whatever came up. He slowly began to feel able not to prepare each session and came to understand that he had used such preparation and holding his ground as a way to both keep people with him in relationship but also at a distance. He realized he had felt the need to be in control in this way, out of fear of others.

Commentary

Peter's therapist understood after a short time that all he needed to do was to talk and that he needed her to listen and to attend. Her attunement to his narrative, to his being, led her to know when to reflect on the conjunction of both what he was talking about, the content, and how he was talking about it, the process. She understood that his desire to keep her involved but at a distance was a necessary but temporary protection, and that the only way to meet this and to understand the intensity of its current counter-productiveness was by being sensitive but direct. This led in its own time to a more dynamic and vibrant, less controlled and less rehearsed relationship.

KEY POINTS

- Dialogue involves openness to alternatives which have not yet been considered while keeping the wider picture in mind.
- Dialogue explores the polarities and paradoxes that underpin human living.
- Dialogue consists of careful description of experience and exploration of its implications, as well as verification of any interpretations put forward.
- Dialogue is about mutuality and collaborative exploration. It is dynamic.
- Clients may not be immediately ready to enter into dialogue, they may initially need silence and find monologue or duologue easier to deal with.

SELF-DISCLOSURE

At the risk of stating the obvious, we are all people; we share the same sorts of hopes and fears, desires and insecurities. This is what the therapist and the client have in common. However, in addition to this basic similarity, by virtue of being in the roles of therapist and client, we are different. Therapist and client are in a formal arrangement whereby one of them, the client, has come to the other, the therapist, to find out something about themselves and their own existence that they did not already know. This creates a tension in therapy that often comes out in the question of self-disclosure.

Existentially, just by being in relationship we disclose ourselves. The location and style of our consulting room, the clothes we wear and the objects we surround ourselves with (or not), all disclose our tastes and lifestyle. As therapists we put ourselves at our clients' disposal and in this process disclose ourselves in everything we do and say or avoid doing and saying. Most often we do all this in ways we are only dimly aware of. Our clients pick up the messages we send out with much greater acuity than we often give them credit for. Of course, we try not to give advice, but clients rarely are in any doubt about what such advice would consist of, if we were to give it.

It is naïve to believe that it is possible to withhold our personality and our worldview and be a neutral presence for the client. It is only natural that in a relationship the two people will be curious about each other. And the client is particularly curious about the therapist, as the latter does not disclose much. Clients will often look up their therapist on the internet and draw their own conclusions. Nevertheless what we disclose about ourselves often gets read in ways we did not expect and such misreadings may be symbolic of the ways the client misreads other people or events around them. We need to be aware of this and work with it.

But requests for disclosures, judgements or opinions from the therapist must be taken carefully with the principle that what is important is what difference it makes for the client to know or not to know about the issue in question. Nevertheless, there may be occasions when not answering a simple question like 'Did you go away in the summer?' may skew the session more than the simple answer, 'Yes I did, thank you.' While remembering that it is the client who is there to talk about what they think, feel and believe, it is often more productive to respond politely to simple questions before asking what made it important for the client to ask the question and how it is different now that they know the answer.

Excessive curiosity about the therapist's actions, thoughts, feelings and beliefs can often be a way of distracting the therapist by overvaluing the therapist's opinion and undervaluing their own and consequently evading their own responsibility as a client. It should be considered and reflected on.

On the other end of the scale are clients who dare not be curious about the therapist. Some clients may find it hard to understand the evidence of the fact that we do take them seriously. Answering further questions about our integrity or significant life events will not give them the answers they need. But further meditation on the reason for needing to know the answer will.

Many of the cases of unethical behaviour heard by professional bodies are of inappropriate disclosure of personal material to the client. Significantly, in most cases the therapist thought they were meeting the needs of the client and were modelling equality. They were not. They were meeting their own needs at the expense of their clients and forgetting what they were there to do: helping the client understand their own lives.

ILLUSTRATION

SELF DISCLOSURE: WHEN IT DID WORK

Sam was a client who had seen his female therapist for nearly six years and who had never really looked at her carefully. He had worked hard in establishing a new sense of selfhood after a total breakdown, which had ended his career as well as landing him in a psychiatric clinic for a while. He had initially been very sceptical of therapy and had been quite reserved, but had gradually unfrozen and taken to the therapeutic process. He had dealt with many complex relationship issues, including his relationship to his mother, his sister, his father and his ex-wife. One day he suddenly, uncharacteristically, looked up at his therapist and said: 'I have just realized you are a woman. This may sound weird, but it has only just occurred to me that you are an actual person. How old are you?' He then blushed and apologized. His therapist responded calmly by telling him her age and remarking that his question, though evidently embarrassing to him, marked an important moment, since he had begun to see her as an other person, a real individual, rather than a simple recipient of his concerns. Sam realized not only how this was indeed significant and new, but also how by his therapist's acknowledgement of his need to start relating in a different way he had taken a first step in a new direction. It was then that he became aware that other people had never truly seemed real to him, as he had only experienced them as either the source of judgements or of care.

Commentary

In this particular situation, the prompt disclosure worked because Sam needed to have a direct response and experience a new way of being with another. The therapist was secure in the knowledge that he was in no way asking this question in order to avoid more important issues, nor that he was playing a social game. He was indeed checking whether his perception about the therapist as a real person was correct. In finding this to be the case he could move forward into a new direction in his other relationships as well. Additionally, he discovered that he had avoided such ways of relating out of fear and out of shame. Both these realizations turned out to be very productive for further work.

ILLUSTRATION

SELF DISCLOSURE: WHEN IT DIDN'T WORK

Beth was seeing a male therapist, who she felt very secure with and who helped her to understand a great deal about her desire to please other people and flatter them. She had just divorced for the second time and was in her early

(Continued)

(Continued)

thirties and childless. After about six months of therapy she asked her therapist whether he had children and was married. Her therapist declined to answer, telling Beth that she was testing the boundaries and that she needed to take responsibility for her desire to get closer to him. This angered Beth and she told him that she had simply asked him a question about his marital status and not whether he wanted to go to bed with her. The therapist now got defensive and made the interpretation that she was being seductive by introducing the topic of having sex with him. Beth felt that this was not only a rejection of her as a woman, but also an accusation of her. She felt her therapist saw her as someone who was loose and provocative and she was greatly upset. At the next session she came back to the issue and her therapist now blankly said: 'Why did you want to know, Beth?' She felt as if whatever she would say next her therapist might construe it as evidence of her suspicious behaviour. She felt trapped and condemned. She broke off the therapy and was angry when her therapist wrote to her to tell her that her breaking off the therapy was evidence of her not accepting that her attempt at seduction had not succeeded.

Commentary

Beth's therapist felt out of his depth when his attractive young client asked him a personal question. He had learnt in his (analytical) training not to answer client questions, but to field them until you could come up with an interpretation instead. This is what he tried to do. When asked why he was so worried about letting his client know that he was also divorced and had two children, who lived with his ex-wife, he realized this was mostly because he feared personalizing the therapy. This was because he felt attracted to the client and had had fantasies of having a relationship with her. His lack of security in the knowledge that he was purely there to help his client understand her world made him over-react to this demand for disclosure. It did not really matter much whether he would or would not tell her what his marital status was. What mattered was whether he could do so without feeling attacked, manipulated or in danger and without for his part wanting to take advantage of the question for personal gain. It is the client's well-being that is the focus of all interaction. And exploration of the answer given or withheld and of the significance of their asking is always better than a defensive or formulaic reply or refusal.

KEY POINTS

- We disclose ourselves by what we say and what we do, by our attitude to others.
- Requests by clients for us to self-disclose can be a way of undermining the therapy work.
- Refusals or agreements to disclose can misfire if they are based on insecurity.
- We need to keep our mind on the client's well-being at all times.

DIRECTIVENESS, DIRECTNESS AND DIRECTION

All this raises the question of whether we are to be directive or non-directive with our clients. There is much confusion about the meaning of these words in psychotherapy. The existential approach is quite clear how it understands them.

When we say that the existential therapist needs to be direct, we mean they need to be purposeful, rather than tactless, straightforward and not obscure, long-winded, or ambiguous. This means, for instance, that they will probably answer a question directly but without saying more than is strictly necessary and that they will not make more than one point in each intervention, that they will not be over-tentative or use theoretical jargon.

The existential therapist does not think in terms of either being directive or non-directive, she aims instead to help the client to find his or her own direction by adhering to the existential principle of respect for the client's autonomy. We do not direct clients, rather we follow their train of thoughts and emotions and show them how to find their own way by self-revelation, self-knowledge, and by finding their own direction in life. As opposed to giving advice, we believe that people learn most from their own experiences by reflecting upon them. At the same time it is important to remember that complete non-directive counselling does not exist because our very presence, not to mention our interventions, provides a new direction for them. When we choose one theme to pick out of the client's story rather than another, we suggest direction. And each time we do not engage with certain ideas they hint at, we block certain paths. We are always directional, but the art is to enable our clients to find direction again, when they had become directionless or rudderless.

Heidegger describes the two basic attitudes a therapist can have towards a client. These are known by the somewhat awkward English translations as 'leaping-in' and 'leaping-ahead'. We have already referred to these in Chapter 2 as 'jumping-in' and 'jumping ahead'. When we jump in, we take over and treat the person as an object. When jumping in, we do not acknowledge the client's autonomy to work out their own direction in life.

When we jump ahead, we are respectful of the client's autonomy. We merely reveal for them a future they may not have been able to conceive of but which is nevertheless implied by their circumstances. We help them to wake up to their own dynamic self-defining potentiality. On many occasions this is unusual for clients and can evoke anxiety. People aren't used to thinking and choosing for themselves, they are used to reacting to others. A client in this position will be likely to ask for advice or suggestions or the therapist's opinion. There are many ways this can be translated into the beginning of direction finding and this can easily be turned into an exercise of exploring options or a playful dreaming about possibilities in an ideal world, followed by reality testing. It is the client's unfolding story that provides the direction, not the therapist's favoured theory, prejudices or their unexamined assumptions about life.

If the principles of freedom and non-intervention are taken too literally, it is easy to stray into non-directiveness and lose our sense of direction as therapists. By doing so we undermine our own autonomy.

Such a *laissez-faire* approach can do as much harm as an autocratic or prescriptive approach. The existential therapist tries to find the balance between directiveness and non-directiveness in order to enable clients to find their own direction in a manner that is surefooted enough to be safe, and challenging enough to provide the excitement of adventure.

On some occasions, however, a client's autonomy may be better acknowledged by being silent and apparently non-interventionist and on other occasions by the therapist being active and apparently quite directive.

Why does a client come back? A client will only come back if they feel that as a result of the experience they have had, they are a little closer to understanding themselves. This happens in the first instance by feeling the therapist has understood them and that the two of them are working in tandem. But this is not enough, they have to feel that the therapist is able to help them grasp something new about life and to help them become good at doing so for themselves. This process of learning to clarify and communicate needs to be started and demonstrated by the therapist. This can be done most effectively by being direct and realistic about what can be offered and by respecting the client's ability to take on this responsibility sooner rather than later. On all occasions, therefore, the therapist will be direct and purposeful and all actions and interventions will be consistent with the principles of phenomenology.

This means that it is systematic but not rigid, responsive but not loose or wild, and clear without being prescriptive. It is essentially always about being fully available and aware and putting one's capacities for understanding at the client's service, so as to help them become more able to understand for themselves.

KEY POINTS

- The existential therapist is purposeful and directional, rather than directive.
- Non-directiveness denies autonomy and can easily lead to stagnation.
- A productive therapeutic relationship will be challenging to both people.
- Clients will value a therapist who is willing to stand with them, but who can also teach them something new about life.

5

FROM THEORY INTO PRACTICE

Knowing is not enough; we must apply. Willing is not enough; we must do.

Goethe

EXPRESSION AND SELF-EXPRESSION: THE PARADOX OF THE SELF

We have already said that the existential approach challenges the idea of a fixed self. We are not fixed, instead we become who we are by the way we live and conduct ourselves. Just as we cannot put a bucket into a fast flowing river and expect the water to have the same quality of movement as it had in the river, the self is inseparable from its life. What we know as the 'self' is the product of the choices and connections we have made and will make. We prefer to talk about a sense of self.

As with the earlier example of the 'mind', it would be more correct to make a verb out of the noun 'self' and to use the verb 'to selve' or the participle 'selving'.

Existentially, the sense of self is the dynamic centre of gravity of a person's network of physical, social, personal and spiritual world relations and these networks are continuously reordered and rebalanced. In this process we are either active or passive. Passivity is an important way of being in terms of resting and replenishing ourselves. But activity is also essential to our survival; as we act on the world, we expand and increase our engagement with the world. The active and passive modes usually balance each other out.

Living passively or reactively comes easily to us, but if it isn't complemented by a more active or even pro-active mode of living which reorganizes, reconsiders and readjusts life, passivity inevitably leads to impasse, and reactivity leads to chaos and confusion.

Living deliberately takes energy, determination and considerable self-scrutiny and consequently we feel less lived by circumstances, less acted on by others, and more alive. In other words we gain a sense of authority, of being the author of our own lives. A sense of self with consistency through time and space is built up by reflecting on our actions.

Physiologically all the cells in our body are being continuously renewed. A blood cell lasts about three months and every one to five years our bones are replaced. This is the way healing occurs, by replacement. The same is true for our sense of self: it shifts and changes a little bit each day and adjusts to new situations. Physiologically we have little difficulty having a feeling of continuity through space and time, but psychologically it seems to be more problematic. And we falsely believe that change is not possible although we often desire it. It may be our default setting motivated by anxiety that stops us being aware of the changes that take place all the time. Existential therapy is a method for enabling people to learn to live deliberately rather than by default. We can learn to be more flexible and freer to let ourselves be transformed by time and circumstances.

The paradox is that we gain a resilient and coherent sense of self *because of* and not *in spite of* our ability to be different in different circumstances.

Questions that may emerge at this point are:

- Am I getting what I want?
- What do I want?
- What do I need to do differently?

ILLUSTRATION

DISCOVERING THE PARADOX OF SELF

Eva was a modest kind of person. For many years she had looked after her family faithfully and well. Peter, her husband of twenty years, was the first to acknowledge Eva's merit and he counted his blessings each day for having married such a wonderful wife and mother to his children. Both Eva and her husband were astonished when Eva had a breakdown, just as both their children were coming to the end of their secondary education and needed their mother's support. Eva and Peter were referred for couple therapy after Eva had consulted a psychiatrist for clinical depression. Though on anti-depressants, she repeatedly stated that she needed Peter to prop her up and sort things out for her. She seemed quite out of touch with herself and her own abilities. She felt incompetent and despairing. The couple work turned into personal therapy in order to allow Eva to work alone and to learn to ask her own questions about her life and her self.

She had no idea who she might be in her own right and what she might be able to contribute to the world beyond her children's education and her husband's need for a 'reliable routine at home'. At first she rejected the very notion that telling her personal story and reflecting on herself might do her any good. Then, gradually she became aware of the emptiness in her life, as her children now had different priorities than being with the family and her husband had become increasingly absorbed by his successful career. Eva began to occupy the therapeutic space with relish as she learnt to play with ideas and with the freedom of experience that human life affords.

Commentary

Eva's therapy rather than focusing on what was wrong with her focused on her ability to think, feel, play, relate and in doing so she rapidly discovered there was a lot more to her than she had ever thought. She became, in her own words, 'a very different person' in a short time. She woke up from the dream of life that had soothed her into the belief that she was just Peter's wife and their children's mother and she came to a new self-awareness, which she found liberating and exhilarating. She returned to higher education and wondered why she had thought she needed anti-depressants, when life itself was so exciting and full of promise. It would have been very easy for the therapy to get bogged down in a pathologized and diminished picture of Eva rather than help her to recover her considerable capacity and vitality.

KEY POINTS

- The self is not something we are given, it is the product of the choices we make.
- Everything we do, every choice we make, is an act of self-expression and self-definition.
- By not choosing to do something or choosing to not do something we diminish ourselves.
- When we reflect on our lives, we have the possibility of gaining a sense of personal responsibility and capacity.
- As human beings we continuously change and this change can be modified in line with our self-reflection.

IDENTIFYING THEMES AND ISSUES

Clients are always talking about what matters to them. They cannot help but show us their concerns and opinions about life because they are alive and their existence matters to them even if they initially do so in a veiled way. It is up to the therapist to learn to listen out for the themes of the client's concerns and preoccupations and to translate these into concrete issues that can be worked on.

But what we mean by an existential theme is not simply that which is being talked about. We mean rather the way a person is engaging with the givens of existence.

We all operate on multiple levels:

- On the physical level, we keep our bodies alive though we all inexorably move towards death.
- On the social level, we try to love and be loved, while invariably we have to learn to deal with opposition and hatred.

- On the personal level, we try to define and establish our identity, while craving and fearing the freedom at the root of our being that affords us more choice than we might like.
- On the spiritual level, we struggle to make sense and understand the world and its contradictions and conflicts while having to tolerate meaninglessness, futility and the relativity of ethics.

For example, if a client talks about feeling intimidated by her partner, while the subject is 'how I get on with my partner', the existential theme emerges from the way in which the issue relates to each of the above, for example:

- In the physical dimension, there may be a feeling of having only a limited time left to live to get the relationship right.
- In the social dimension, there may be a feeling of not deserving a relationship of mutuality.
- In the personal dimension, there may be a feeling of not being able to make an autonomous decision to choose what sort of relationship to be in.
- In the spiritual dimension, there may be a nagging doubt about how to decide what is right and wrong, not knowing how to evaluate whether or how this relationship is helpful or harmful.

Existential concerns are frequently signalled by their absence so one of the ways in which a theme can be represented is by not being talked about. Something may impact on people without them realizing it. People are often not used to thinking and talking about things in that way. Or they may simply never have come across the issue that they are missing. For instance, a young adult, raised in a family where efficiency and academic performance ruled, may not realize that affection and devotion to another human being make emotional demands that will also add great value. Problems with intimacy with a partner show up this blind spot at the core of existence and a client's perplexity and confusion about their feelings will lead to the need for new discoveries around the existential theme of relationship.

Working with themes and issues

Remembering that existence embraces all of these dimensions simultaneously, the therapist can note how much of the dialogue is focussed on one or another, or which of them are rarely referred to and wonder:

- How is a theme represented within the present topic?
- How are the givens being evaded or denied?
- How is the client trying to become alive and fulfilled?
- What are the risks and how are they being avoided?
- How resilient are the themes and which situations do they occur in and not occur in?
- What does the theme say about the client's worldview and their experience of life?

The existential therapist will remember to keep all interventions anchored in present experience, and not to intellectualize or abstract too much. They will phenomenologically draw the client's attention to the presence or absence of the theme.

Simply identifying the issues is likely to be of relatively little value on its own, and the client may feel the therapist is just picking elements out of their story and not understand why. It will be of greater value if the therapist can refer to the paradox and dilemma embedded in the way the issue is talked about, as in: 'On the one hand you like being single, but on the other you have rarely been out of a relationship. Can you tell me a bit more about this? It suggests a certain tension or even a contradiction in your life.'

ILLUSTRATION

CLARIFYING AND WORKING WITH THEMES AND ISSUES

Mike was a 42-year-old man with a successful career who loved driving his convertible at speeds well beyond the legal limit. He had numerous male friends and colleagues that he got on with fairly well and considered himself popular, not just for taking people out for a spin or for drinks (and offering to pay). Yet he found it very hard to approach women 'to go out with him'. He was quite talkative and reflective about many events and experiences he had during the day at work, but remained aloof about a fact of his life that only emerged at the third session, which was that he still lived with his parents and had never lived independently. Initially it was taboo to bring this issue up for discussion and he did not want any help in tackling the autonomy issues he was avoiding. It was only when the therapist had the wisdom of pointing out that he was keen to claim his independence of mind and that he was adamant about making his own decisions about which problems to bring or resolve, that Mike suddenly unfroze and began to consider the ways in which his lifestyle hampered this autonomy. It then became clear that he was deeply ashamed of his dependency and that it was this that prevented him inviting women out as well, since he feared having to admit to them that he would not be able to take them 'home to his pad', but would have to introduce them directly to his parents instead. It was the very fact of facing these issues and speaking them out loud for the first time that made a difference to Mike's sense of who he was. He knew immediately that he did not want to carry on sticking his head in the sand or hanging it in shame. He wanted to hold his head high instead and have his own place, in which he could choose to do as he wished, especially with women. It occurred to him that his car was nothing but a toy and that he had never really given himself a chance to grow up, preferring to play with toys instead. He sold his car and used the money as a down payment on his own flat. His life quickly transformed after that initial step towards independence and maturity.

Commentary

The therapist, picking up on Mike's reluctance to invite women out, might have fallen into various interpretive traps, such as suggesting that Mike might prefer

(Continued)

(Continued)

male over female company and that he might be struggling with his sexual identity. Or she might have assumed that Mike was afraid of female attention because his mother had been a castrating influence. In reality, Mike was well aware of what he called 'his cowardice in self-indulgently remaining in the family home'. It was embarrassment at this lazy habit that had made him keep women at bay and that undermined his self-esteem.

KEY POINTS

- Existential themes are present in all human issues.
- Awareness of the themes can be used by the therapist to make sense of different aspects of the client's narrative.
- Clients invariably feel a great sense of relief when they begin to tackle existential themes that have hitherto been hidden or out of sight.
- The initiative needs to come from the client rather than from the therapist, but the therapist's search for clarification will often prompt this development and will focus understanding of it.

IDENTIFYING VALUES AND BELIEFS

The word 'values' refers quite simply to what we give value to, what is important to us and we appreciate. Values are present in all human events. We like to think of them as fixed and beyond discussion and certainly feel more secure if we can do so. But actually they arise out of our understanding of particular personal and social experiences and then evolve into apparently fixed laws.

Values are the connecting threads that give us a feeling of integrity and connectivity and constitute the framework of meaning that make our lives worthwhile. Our task as human beings is to come up with a value system which is resilient, coherent and robust, yet also flexible enough to live by and to adapt to new circumstances. Many clients talk about lacking this sense of rightness and sureness of direction in life.

One of the values of existential therapy is that people are encouraged to discover and live by their own value system, to understand why it is important and why they have chosen it and how it ties them in with the people around them and connects them deeply to those they love.

Our task as therapists is sometimes to challenge the robustness or rigidity of our clients' values.

Values and beliefs are the basis of a personal code of ethics which is about:

- how I want to live my life;
- how I want to treat others and be treated by others;

- how I evaluate my actions and those of others;
- how I feel about human existence as a result;
- how I evolve a sense of overall purpose and meaning.

Everything we do indicates something about our personal value system and all of our actions are based on our beliefs and values. To put it even more simply, our values are at the root of why we get up in the morning and how well we sleep at night.

Whereas themes and issues will generally be explicit, values and beliefs will be more implicit because they relate to the spiritual dimension of existence, the *Überwelt*. In therapy, though, the focus is always on the client's specific experience and the way in which their implicit beliefs and values determine the way they live their lives. More often than not, clients have been unaware of the impact their values have on their lives.

Existentially we can only be in a position to choose our own values if we can live with the anxiety of there being no absolute values. Therefore the existential therapist will need to be prepared to question and challenge values. We can only do this if we have come to know the meaning of our own values first. It is essential that our values ultimately are arrived at as a result of personal choice and reflection rather than by default or by following the crowd.

Working with the client's value system

We all have to live with value systems that we did not choose and on many occasions we adopt one which is familiar to us. No one likes to have their values questioned but occasionally something happens in life that forces us to question them. Clients often come to therapy at a time when their values are under question. This evokes great anxiety because they realize perhaps for the first time that it is up to them to make sense of a world they have grown out of touch with. In the process of re-evaluating a value system it will be necessary to decide how much something is worth – what its value is – and whether something is worth sacrificing something else for.

We need to consider:

- Which values are useful now? Which belong to an earlier time of life?
- What feelings and life worlds are evoked by the value?
- What contradictions exist between the different values a client has and how they live them?
- Which values have been accepted without reflection and choice and which have not?
- What does it mean to a person to define themselves as the sort of person who believes and values what they do?

Because values are implicit, we are more likely to find out about a client's value system from their relationships, thoughts and fears and the consequences of their actions than by asking about them directly. Another clue is the way they talk. People say things like: 'It's just not right when …' or 'It's not fair that …'. Using the word 'should' also indicates a value. These can be looked at phenomenologically, noticing the beliefs and assumptions the person holds. We should not be surprised initially to hear responses like 'Well, it just is, it's obvious isn't it?' It may seem obvious to a person that something is the case when in fact it is not, because they have simply not reflected on it. Existential therapists do not proscribe or prescribe values, they point out to clients where their values become apparent and how such values may lead to contradictions or tensions with other givens of reality.

EXERCISE

Think of a time when you were forced to re-think your values on an important issue. What did you feel, think, do and learn before, during and after the event?

Many issues clients bring are about conflicts between their own values or between their own and other people's value systems. For example, a person may want to buy something for themselves, but feel that they should be saving the money to spend on their family. There is a conflict of values between spending on oneself and spending on others. This conflict needs to be examined, and underlying this specific conflict we may find a deeper conflict between, for instance, our desire to be liked by others and our desire for things we like. All the assumptions underlying such conflicts can be examined and if clients do not bring up their unease with their values and beliefs, it may be necessary to bring it to their attention.

Clients who are in a crisis or in the middle of a process of transformation often need time to come to terms with their changing values and allow themselves to think differently about life and replace old values with new ones.

EXERCISE

- What is it like when you meet a client who has the same value system as you?
- What is it like when you meet a client who has a value system you strongly disagree with?
- What makes you think that your value system is best, and how will this enable or interfere with your ability to listen to your client?

Every relationship is an example of what happens when one value system meets another and sometimes a client's struggle with conflicting values is echoed by the therapist's own struggle. Such clashes need to be brought to supervision or personal therapy. Training is about recognizing value-based contradictions and learning to handle them, remembering they can never be eliminated.

Sometimes it is difficult not to react to what a client says with either 'that's right' or 'that's bad' or some such. These are clues to your own values which need to be acknowledged, owned and bracketed so they do not contaminate your listening too much. With experience, this becomes easier.

In therapy, the client may disagree with some of your stated values, for instance, with your policy of paying for missed sessions. The issue is not whether they agree or disagree, but the dilemma of managing difference. The alternative is that the disagreements are denied and so become cemented by strong defensive and self-protective feelings on both sides. This will ultimately lead to the breakdown of the therapeutic relationship. Therapy is a place to reflect on the consequent feelings, thoughts and actions. Clients and therapists will always have differences of opinion and acknowledging this helps the therapeutic relationship to become real. Sometimes clients find this too threatening and will pretend the therapist has the same view as they do. Sometimes therapists find it too threatening to openly discuss their values and set their own views aside in order to accommodate the client. It takes a lot to be at ease with conflict and difference and to be able to meet differences without struggle but with fairness and clarity. This is an essential part of therapy training.

If both therapist and client are open and flexible enough, they will find a new ever more apt value system to live by. It is not unusual for a therapist to begin questioning their own values while being confronted with a client's life crisis that evokes anxiety in both of them and which requires a review of what is right and wrong, real and imagined.

ILLUSTRATION

BEING CONFRONTED BY VALUES AND BELIEFS

Mark, a psychotherapist, rode his bicycle everywhere and never wore a helmet, giving the reason to his many questioners that it probably would not make any difference and that he did not like the feel of it. He liked the freedom of being on his bike and quite resented people's questions and challenges of his habit. He valued his independence of thought and action. Coming back from work one dark evening only two hundred yards from home, he came off his bike and hit his head on the road. The next thing he knew was coming round in his local hospital to the sound of the doctors talking to each other about his injuries. He had been unconscious for about 45 minutes. Considering the circumstances, his injuries were comparatively superficial. When he recovered, he carried on riding his bike but bought a helmet.

Commentary

Reflecting afterwards on this unforeseen brush with death forced him to reassess his value system. He acknowledged that his situation in life was not simply as an individual, but as a member of a family and that his wife and children (among

(Continued)

(Continued)

others) would be affected by anything that happened to him and moreover that he was responsible for more than he had previously acknowledged, including his clients. He realized that he was no use to himself or them if he was dead. After the accident his interconnectedness with them was more tangible. The situation he had been in when he had made the original choice to maintain independence of thought and action and which subsequently gave rise to the decision not to wear a helmet was made in childhood under rather different circumstances, but still adhered to and there had never previously been an occasion that called it into question. This original decision was revisited and he realized he could make a new more context-consistent choice without being compelled to. This new choice involved a sacrifice but this was valued as being worth it. While he was generally aware of the unpredictability of other road users and of pedestrians, he could not take account of contingency. His situation, the givens of existence and his responsibility came into focus in a near-death encounter and the effect was transformative. This encounter enabled him to be more open to clients who were confronted by contingency and chance such that they had to reconsider their value system.

KEY POINTS

- A person's values are about what they consider valuable to them.
- It is always useful and often transformative to reflect on the values we live by.
- Many of a person's values were decided long ago. It is important to consider which are useful now and occasionally re-evaluate.
- People often experience anxiety and confusion when there is a contradiction between their values and the actions they take.
- Any change in values involves a sacrifice.
- Values are what tie us in with other people.

EMOTIONS AS A COMPASS

Emotions have a central position in existential therapy because emotional experience has the most direct connection with our intentional nature. Feelings are neither solely caused by the world nor are they solely independent of the world. Emotions are far more than simply physiological. They are constant reminders of what matters to us and what we value. They are the evidence of our resonance with the world, with others and with the principles we live by. But this is not to say that emotions are simple or that their meaning is always obvious. Emotions are the ebb and flow of human experience with currents and undercurrents and cross-currents. They are like the weather and there is never no weather.

A radical difference between the existential and some other traditions is that existentially we consider that there are no intrinsically positive or negative emotions. Whether we label them as positive or negative is simply a measure of how comfortable or unfamiliar they are and whether they lead us in the direction of what we value or what we dread. Emotions locate us within our existence and offer us both possibility and necessity of action, responsibility and choice.

But there is a paradox too, that while they point us towards what matters, they can also blind us to alternatives. For example, if I feel fearful about an aspect of my life, I will tend to see that aspect of the world as frightening and reduce any other way of interpreting the world.

Because emotions are connected to our basic dilemmas, we never have just one feeling about an event. We usually have a mixture of emotions. We might feel hope *and* fear, are excited *and* overwhelmed, feel guilt *and* anger *and* sadness. This can be very confusing to many people.

Someone who has trust in their emotional life will have a way of guiding themselves through life's unpredictability while savouring the feelings it throws up. Someone who loses the ability to trust their emotions ends up denying them, and by doing so, denying themselves and their existence. They become empty and feel like nothing and literally no longer know who they are.

At the other end of the scale are people who are thrown about by too much emotion. Their emotions may become so magnified that they prevent good contact with the world and especially with other people, but also with themselves.

Therapy is a time when our emotions may become explicitly clarified. As they become more obvious and more articulate, they help us find new direction in life.

The aim of existential psychotherapy is to learn how we resonate with the events in our world and to learn the significance of the consequent moods and emotions.

Working with emotions

In order to make it easier to work actively with emotions in therapy, we can use what we call the emotional compass (Figure 5.1), which can help us recognize the quality and meaning of an emotion as well as the value they point to and the direction of our emotional movements. The magnetic North on this compass indicates the direction of our aspiration and goal. When we achieve this, we call this happiness. The opposite Pole on the compass indicates the bottom line of our experience when we are as far removed from achieving our objectives as we can imagine. This rock bottom position is often experienced as depression. The Eastern region, when going down from the North to the South is where we resist change and fight against being deprived of what we value. The epitome of this experience is that of anger. The Western region, going up towards that which we aspire to, is the experience of hope, where we feel we may actually ascend to the position of happiness. The various in-between emotions are described below. Of course there are many complex variations in emotional tonality and the subtleties of our emotions are important to trace and become familiar with. The compass merely gives a general sense of direction and increases our understanding of the whereabouts of any specific feeling on the general spectrum of emotions. It helps us to make sense of the flow of emotions and to accept that they are not

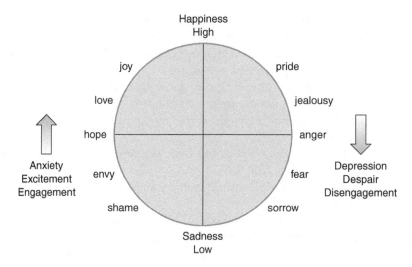

Figure 5.1   The compass of emotions

random, nonsensical or static. Emotions are not just a nuisance, even though clients are likely to come to therapy because they see their emotions as static and bothersome, obstructing their life. We need to help them to get moving again in their emotions and to understand the message their feelings are sending them.

All emotions point towards a value and indicate the nature of our anxiety or despair about it. Starting from the top right we can make sense of each emotion as relating to the value we are trying to achieve and maintain.

- *Pride* shows a certain taking for granted of what we value and enjoy. As the saying goes, it almost certainly comes before a fall. It feels like confidence, but may look to others like arrogance.
- *Jealousy* shows that what we value and enjoy is under threat and we try to guard it desperately, lest we may lose it. It feels like cautiousness but may look like possessiveness.
- *Anger* shows our sense that what we value is dangerously threatened and that we feel entitled to try to retrieve it with a final push of energetic effort. It feels like self-assertion but may look like aggression.
- *Fear* indicates that we do not believe we can save that which we value, and that we want to remove ourselves from the threat to our prized possession. The experience of loss takes over from that of possession. It may feel like self-preservation, but may look like cowardice.
- *Sorrow* is the expression of loss and shows that we are letting go of the valued possession, letting ourselves become empty of it. This leads us back to the rock bottom position of depression, where we may well be tempted to wallow for a while, since it affords a paradoxical safety and a state of giving up which may lead to apathy. It feels like pain, but may come across as giving up.
- *Shame* indicates that we still experience the emptiness of loss but that we have begun to swing back upwards. We are comparing ourselves to what might be and

we already aspire to regaining what we value or gaining a new value, but we are failing to achieve this for the moment. We feel ashamed at our own lack, though this may jolt us in to action. It feels like inferiority but may look like guilt.

- *Envy* indicates our aspiration to achieve a new value without a definite sense of whether it will be concretely feasible to do so. This is the experience of recognition of the value we aspire to in others, without as yet believing that this is achievable for us. This is the forerunner of our ability to recover our own desire. It feels like desire, but may look like rivalry.
- *Hope* is our awareness of the possibility that we may actually be able to attain that which is valued, while still maintaining a fair distance from actual possession of the object. We now have a firm objective as well as the belief that we might even achieve this. It feels like courage but may look like wishful thinking.
- *Love* is the experience of going out of ourselves towards that which is prized in a commitment of care for it: our intentionality fixed deliberately and clearly on the object of value and an engagement with what it takes to stay true to it. It feels like passion but may come across as obsession.
- *Joy* is the emotion that accompanies our grateful achievement of what we value, in a movement of unification. It feels like pleasure, but may look like giddiness. It leads to happiness over having achieved what we most valued. This may turn to a certain complacency and pride, so that the cycle can start all over again.

Clients often talk about their feelings in particular ways:

- as constraints on their freedom – 'I want to go see my mother but I feel too angry.'
- as too much – 'I've been feeling very emotional in the last few weeks.'
- as too little – 'I can't get excited about anything.'
- as not rational – 'It doesn't make sense, I don't know why I'm feeling like this.'
- as not mine – 'My partner makes me feel so angry.'
- as needing to be controlled – 'I just need to get a grip on how I feel, I just need to stop it.'
- as having the wrong ones – 'I need to stop feeling so resentful and start feeling happier.'
- as either positive or negative – 'I want to have some better feelings, I shouldn't be feeling like this.'

All these indicate that their significance is not fully understood, since each of our emotions is valid and has a story to tell us.

Sensations, feelings, thoughts and intuitions

Emotions are the more complex as we may be confused between different sorts of feelings, or indeed between sensations, feelings, thoughts and intuitions:

1   Sensations are what we pick up at bodily level, derived from the five senses: hearing, sight, smell, touch and taste. These experiences are translated into feelings as soon as the brain receives the message, which is experienced as pleasant or unpleasant, as pleasure or pain. A lot of our feelings come through our senses which tell us whether we like or dislike something.

2   Feelings is a word often equated with the experience of our emotional life, when we express or suppress the emotions described above, often without realizing what they are about. We can learn to recognize how such feelings are always about attraction or repulsion in relation to what is most valued.

3   Thoughts can intervene to describe or make judgements about our sensations and feelings. They can help us articulate what we feel and make sense of it. Sometimes thoughts take over from sensations and feelings, so that we get out of touch with what we really experience.

4   Intuitions are the way in which we directly apprehend the value of things in an immediate appraisal of the sum total of the input of our five senses, our complex emotional response and the fleeting thoughts that remain unarticulated. We need to learn to make use of all of these forms of conscious awareness.

Sensations and feelings relate respectively to bodily and emotional experience, whereas thoughts are generally attempts to explain, and intuitions are evaluations of our experience. It is most helpful to learn to tune into all of these different dimensions of being in the world. As sensations become sharper, feelings become more articulated and in turn this leads to awareness of more deeply held thoughts and values.

It helps for therapists to elicit all of these experiences and it generally works better if they refer to feelings as 'important' or 'significant' rather than as 'interesting'. 'Important' or 'significant' indicates presence of passion, whereas 'interesting' indicates something worthy of note but of no great meaning.

ILLUSTRATION

FEELING AND THINKING

Compare these two responses:

1. Feeling

Therapist: How did you feel when he said that to you?
Client: Upset.
Therapist: How do you mean?
Client: Well, angry really, angry with him and angry with myself.
Therapist: What's that like?
Client: Really frustrating … I want to scream.
Therapist: Can you say a bit more about how that feels?
Client: Strangely powerful, but scary too.
Therapist: Two very important feelings.
Client: Yes, familiar too.

2. Thinking

Therapist: What did you think when he said that to you?
Client: I didn't like it.
Therapist: Do you know why?
Client: Not really, except that I usually feel upset when I'm ignored.
Therapist: Why is that?
Client: It's because I was often ignored in the past.
Therapist: You think that may be the reason?
Client: Yes maybe that could explain a few things.
Therapist: About how you came to be this way?
Client: Yes, maybe. It's interesting, I suppose.

Commentary

By concentrating on the feeling dimension of experience, within a short space of time the client was able to engage with a deeper level of experience, in contrast with the thinking responses which stay at a theoretical level. Note the use of the words 'important' and 'interesting'.

Emotions and phenomenology

Description needs to focus initially on emotional experience, rather than on mediated intellectual or cognitive experience. This captures the immediacy of our experience, leading to a fuller understanding of our nature and the limitations we impose on ourselves. Explanations lead away from such understanding.

Particularly at the beginning of therapy we can use our own knowledge of situations similar to those the client is describing to get some clues about what it may be like. In such situations it is better to be phenomenological and ask yourself and your client: 'How did you experience this?', 'What was that like?' or 'What did that feel like?'. You are checking out and eliciting description, rather than speculating and jumping to conclusions like: 'You must have been angry'.

The first response, 'How did you experience this?' will enable you to get a better idea of how the client experiences him or herself and also how accurately we can get into their world. If we predict they will say 'angry' and they say 'afraid', we have learnt a great deal about our ability to imagine our self into their world.

The last response, 'You must have been angry', although possibly correct, can act as a suggestion to someone who has a tentative or reduced emotional vocabulary. If they are unsure about what word to use, they may take your suggestion as an instruction without really knowing what it means. Also it shuts down the possibility of there being other less obvious feelings.

It is often good to simply enquire: 'What was that like for you?' or to ask what a person's experience of something is, rather than focus exclusively on their feeling.

The point is to encourage your client to feel their way into their own experience, get in touch with it, describe it, validate it, understand it and find a way to deal with it.

EXERCISE

Thinking about your life, make three lists of feelings you have:

1 those you have frequently;
2 those you have occasionally;
3 those you rarely have.

- What occurs to you about these lists?
- How did you learn the words for your feelings?
- What attitudes do you have towards those you rarely have?
- Were the feelings sensations, emotions, thoughts or intuitions?

Awareness of your client's emotional vocabulary

We must always remember that a person's emotional vocabulary, the words they use to represent their emotional life, will be constrained by their personal and cultural experience and that their vocabulary is unlikely to represent their breadth of experience adequately. There are many dozens of words used to refer to feelings and some will be more easily named and owned than others. Whether the therapist or client speaks in their first language makes a difference to how their feelings are experienced and understood. Speaking in a second language can place a limitation on how strongly feelings can be expressed or even experienced. Different cultures favour different emotional registers. Often feelings that cannot be experienced will be acted on instead. A client who is angry with their therapist may find it easier to miss the next session. We need to be aware of this and be prepared to raise it.

ILLUSTRATION

SPEAKING IN A SECOND LANGUAGE

Client: ... and that's why I came to this country, I needed to get away.

Therapist: How do you mean?

Client: Because I hate everything Italian, I've always loved the English and speaking English.

Therapist: What is it about speaking English?

Client: I can forget things.

Therapist: Like what?

Client: How I felt growing up, feeling confused, lost ... you know, I've just realized that I've never said 'Ti amo', I still can't, I used to hate it when my parents said it, but I can say 'I love you' easily. Why is that?

Therapist.	I don't know, what occurs to you?
Client.	It helps me to distance myself from the feelings?
Therapist.	Could be, how does it feel saying it?
Client.	Yes, it feels much more difficult saying it, and hearing it too, much more vulnerable.

Therapists need to ask themselves:

• To what extent do I or my clients have access to the full range of emotions?
• How broad is the client's emotional vocabulary?
• What words do they use a lot?
• What words do they hardly use at all?

Tracing emotions back to dilemmas

The object for the therapist is always for their interventions to promote a stronger engagement with the complexity of emotional experience. Invariably the therapist will ask questions in the present tense as in 'What is that like?' rather than the past tense 'What was it like?'

This will help the person focus in on the essential aspects of the dilemma, and this can be followed up with interventions like: 'What about that is important?' or 'How is that relevant to you at this moment?' or 'What does that mean to you?' This tracing back is adventurous and challenging for both the therapist and client and will usually reveal a dilemma which can be expressed as: 'On the one hand you feel [angry] and on the other hand you feel [scared]. How does that feel?'

These double-sided values need to be faced so that the tension that is generated can be used more productively. Ultimately such dilemmas are only resolvable by choice. The purpose of tracing back through the emotions is to ensure that the consequent choice is made in circumstances of greater freedom and knowledge than previously. Emotions connect to actions.

By tracing back to the original intention we will be able to consider:

• What led me to do that?
• What I am doing this for and how do I want to approach this new situation in my life so that it becomes a building block of the future I want for myself?
• What will be the consequence of me acting this way or that in relation to this emotion and the value it points towards?'

Although this will often lead to catharsis, to an expression of emotions, it will only lead to insight if the feelings are worked with so that they become familiar and are understood. As always, the feelings will lead to a more profound recognition of current values and beliefs.

ILLUSTRATION

THE EFFECT OF WORKING WITH EMOTIONS

Kate came to therapy on the suggestion of a friend. She had been having 'panic attacks' and the friend suggested she learn some techniques for managing them. She was told it would only take a few sessions to learn them. The therapist began by asking her to recount the situations in which she had the panic attacks and she described them in a very matter-of-fact way: 'I was walking along on the way to work and suddenly I couldn't breathe and thought I was going to faint.' She did not know what was happening and her friend told her it was a panic attack. In answer to an enquiry about how it felt, she said, 'I don't know … what do you mean? … I just felt I couldn't breathe.' Subsequent sessions focussed on her emotional vocabulary which was very small. She described other situations past and present where she had somehow skipped over awareness of how she felt in favour of noticing what she thought or what she believed she should think. At the beginning of the work she would come in and read her diary of the week's events, which was extensive, but which left little room for dialogue. She gradually did this less and less and came in one session saying that she had had a revelation. She said: 'You know, I've just realized something, and I don't know why I never knew this, but my feelings are not things I have, they are what I am, and that makes them OK, doesn't it.' She said this as a statement, not a question.

Commentary

Family life in Kate's early years had involved much expression of feelings but little reflection on them. She had consequently not developed an awareness of her emotional life or an emotional vocabulary. She had, however, developed ways of managing or suppressing them which had been largely successful until the 'panic attacks', when they spilled over. Therefore she wanted other ways of managing them. She was fortunately sufficiently curious about her psychological life to follow her therapist's request to openly explore the meaning of her feelings and their relative absence. Although it took some months, she was able to arrive at a point where she could understand the message of her emotions specifically and also generally in such a way that she was able to own them in their dynamic complexity.

KEY POINTS

- Our emotions are like a compass and are what connects us and locates us within our existence. They point us towards what matters.
- Emotions are not things we have, they are aspects of how we are.
- Emotions are more complex than our vocabulary leads us to believe.

- Focussing on feelings can help us pinpoint what it is that matters and makes life meaningful.
- When understood our feelings help us to decide on our actions.

CHOICE AND RESPONSIBILITY

The word choice is used a lot in everyday life, but what it means to choose and what it means to select are often muddled. Selection is when we decide between options. These may be options of partners, holiday destinations or items on a menu. Existentially, choosing means to own the decision one has just taken. In everyday life we may not have a number of options before us, but we still have an existential choice and that is whether to own or disown our course of action. As Shakespeare's Hamlet says, 'To be or not to be, that's the question' (*Hamlet* 3.1). Indeed, existentially there is only one question, whether to embrace life and the consequences of our actions, or whether to evade and deny it. The former will lead to a greater and more passionate engagement with life and the latter will lead to a lesser engagement and a sense of pretence that it is not really happening or that others are to blame for what goes wrong in life. It may also lead to us opting out entirely.

Therefore, passively not choosing has just as strong a consequence as any active choice we may make. We have already seen how we are constrained by the givens of existence in general and the conditions of our own personal existence in particular. These are the boundaries that guide our choices.

We can never blame anyone else for our actions and their consequences. We live on our own account. This also applies to the positives that occur: if we can own them, we cannot dismiss these as merely fortuitous and we can then take some credit for making them happen.

The philosopher at the end of Woody Allen's film *Crimes and Misdemeanors* says:

> We are all faced throughout our lives with agonizing decisions and choices. Some of these are on a grand scale, some are on a lesser scale, but we define ourselves by the choices we make. We are in fact the sum total of these choices.

What this means is that everything we do is in some way chosen. Even not choosing is a choice and has a consequence. There is no way of avoiding this challenge that life presents. Our freedom to choose releases us from determinism and allows us to embrace responsibility for ourselves on the basis of our choices. It is a given.

Working with choice and responsibility

An underlying principle of all existential work is to introduce, or re-introduce the client to the reality that not only did they contribute to the situation in which they find themselves now but that they can also take responsibility for it changing.

ILLUSTRATION

WORKING WITH CHOICE AND COMMITMENT

Paul referred himself for what he called 'careers counselling'. The issue was, as he put it, whether to stay in his present job or to move to a new one. He couldn't decide and wanted to think through his options. It seemed to him that all he needed was to get a clearer idea of the pros and cons of each job and then the answer would be made for him. At the end of each session, he came to a conclusion, only to reverse it by the next session. He didn't understand what he was doing wrong. He said, apparently flippantly, 'If only the decision could be made for me.' He realized that job choices in the past had always been made for him.

It was put to him that perhaps there was something else going on that was not necessarily anything to do with the relative merits of the two jobs and was more to do with the consequences of not choosing. He reluctantly agreed, saying that he did not want to give up either. 'For what do I do if I'm wrong,' he said, 'it'll be my fault then'. 'As it will if you don't decide,' his counsellor said. The turning point, which did not come suddenly, was when he realized not choosing was just as much of a decision, and also one that he did not feel proud of. 'Whichever choice I take, go, stay or procrastinate, it's me that takes it, and each one involves rejecting another.'

Commentary

Paul moved from a point where he saw making decisions as being a technical exercise of adding up objective pros and cons which had implications of certainty and predictability, to one where he was going to have to risk the unknown and reap the consequences. The pay-off, whether 'successful' or 'unsuccessful', would be the same, which was that he would gain a greater sense of autonomy and ownership of his life. This would be scary or exciting depending on how he chose to look at it.

KEY POINTS

- Choice is about owning rather than disowning the consequences of our actions.
- We need to learn what we can realistically take responsibility for and what we cannot.
- When we become aware of the risks involved in living, we may be able to liberate ourselves of our fears and dare to live with anxiety.
- The ability to take responsibility for our actions will lead to the realisation that persistence, and not luck, will lead to success

ANXIETY: AUTHENTICITY, GUILT AND BAD FAITH

Although we may not actively think about the givens of existence all the time, there are constant reminders in everyday life. Illness reminds us of frailty and mortality, loss of relationships remind us of our isolation and our need for others, events not going the way we planned remind us of freedom and chance, and discovering our beliefs about existence are simply that – beliefs and not facts, reminds us of meaninglessness and uncertainty.

These dilemmas of life niggle at us at least in part because they are unsolvable and we like to be able to complete tasks. They evoke a sort of background hum which, try as we might, we cannot ignore. They are the uncertain background to our lives that we describe as existential anxiety.

As practitioners we need to distinguish this existential or ontological anxiety, from everyday personal responses to specific events. Such responses like stress, agitation, phobias, depression, sleeplessness or addiction take their hidden power from the underlying awareness of the fragility of our existence and feed off our fundamental existential anxiety. It can be said that one-third of suffering is ontological and the other two-thirds occur because we cannot accept the one-third. Each everyday anxiety is a pointer to existential anxiety. It is illustrated by Bill Watterson (1995) in his Calvin and Hobbes comic strip (Figure 5.2).

Figure 5.2 The unsettling nature of existential anxiety

Reflecting on existence inevitably brings anxiety which we can either embrace or evade and deny. Each option has its consequences:

- The consequence of embracing anxiety is a feeling of aliveness, excitement and is the source of creativity. It is ambition. To want to do something you haven't done before and not be afraid to take a risk with life and face the consequences. This is authenticity and this meaning of authenticity has nothing to do with what is genuine or closest to the true self. Existentially since there is no essence for the person to be true to, we cannot talk about a person being authentic. Authenticity is the English translation of a term used by Heidegger (*Eigentlichkeit*, which means ownness or actuality), and the biggest clue to the existential meaning of authenticity is in the first four letters 'auth' as in authorship. It refers to how much a person is able to be open to existence, anticipate its truth, oversee its difficulties and take responsibility for the consequences of their choices. Authenticity cannot be standardized or normalized. What makes an action authentic is whether it is chosen and owned in full knowledge of the situation and the potential consequences. Authentic living is aware living.

• The consequence of evasion and denial is equivalent to evading and denying life. The path of least resistance leads to the place of least existence. This is inauthenticity and is about denial of authorship and personal responsibility. A characteristic of inauthentic living is that one sees oneself as being caused, and life as a technical problem to be solved. It is often about doing what we imagine will please others or doing what we think is expected of us.

Both options are hard to sustain for any length of time, and for this reason we prefer to talk about the single idea of authenticity/inauthenticity. There is always some amount of each in our attitude. Sometimes we need to keep our heads down and be inauthentic. Sometimes we are able to truly embrace life and be for real.

Authenticity can only be an aim of psychotherapy as long as we remember the following:

• That it is a general statement of intent and direction rather than an expectation of a particular end result.
• It is not a norm.
• We can never rid ourselves of inauthenticity, and any claims to have done so are inauthentic themselves.

The sort of unease that inauthenticity leads to is called existential guilt. This is different from everyday guilt when we do something we should not have done. It is also different from neurotic guilt when we imagine we have done something wrong simply because we have learnt to be afraid of our own freedom to act. Existential guilt is when we realize we have failed to achieve our potential and could have done more. This happens when we lie to ourselves. It is self-deception. Sartre calls it bad faith which is the denial of our freedom and responsibility. It happens when we deny that something is true when it is, or pretend that something is true when it isn't. It often means that we do not act when we know we should, or we pretend there is nothing we can do about a situation when there is something we can do. It is a background awareness that we are continuously responsible for our lives.

Existential Therapy needs to have these preoccupations as the backdrop to the therapy work. Figure 5.3 illustrates how people continuously move through a cycle of inauthenticity and authentic awareness.

Working with authenticity and inauthenticity

In therapy, the relative presence or absence of authenticity can be seen in the way the client denies freedom and responsibility for her life, or takes responsibility for someone

Figure 5.3   The existential cycle of authenticity

else's. The existential therapist will be alert to these and when the time is right draw them to the client's attention.

- **Pronoun switching.** This is when the personal pronoun 'I' is substituted with other pronouns or other people. The intention is to make the issue less personally meaningful by pushing the immediacy of the feeling away. Often the personal 'I' will change to a more impersonal 'you', 'he', 'she', 'they', 'people' when the issue becomes more sensitive.
- **Excessive referring to the past,** as in wanting to tell the therapist what has happened to them in the past, to the exclusion of what is happening to them now or what they wish to achieve in the future. This can include justifying the present in terms of the past as in 'I am like this because of what happened to me'.
- **Excessive referring to the future,** as in concentrating on what will happen, usually at a time not in the immediate future. It can also include making plans which rarely get put into action or evaluated. This is a form of wishful thinking.

- **Being reactive rather than active,** as in seeing themselves as determined by others and waiting to see what someone else in their life will do before making a decision about what they want.
- **Seeing the therapist as the authority.** This has two dimensions, first, as an authority to rely on. This can come out by the client asking for advice about what to do, or trying to tap the therapist's theoretical knowledge, or by agreeing with everything the therapist says. These can all be hard to resist, especially the last, because we all like to think that our interventions are accurate. We must remember that we are not right all the time and what we aim for is a discussion about the issues, not agreement that we are correct. The second dimension is when the client is intimidated by the therapist's authority and is excessively wary of revealing anything for fear of judgement.
- **The therapist's contribution.** The therapist has to live with authenticity/inauthenticity but also be aware of it. Pronoun switching, referring to the past or the future inappropriately, and feeling reactive are all ways the therapist can reduce her effectiveness. In addition, there is a danger of the therapist using her authority to impose her knowledge and power. Similarly, denying the authority of her knowledge and experience will lead to a less effective therapeutic relationship.

ILLUSTRATION

PRONOUN SWITCHING

Client: ... and then she shouted at me.

Therapist: Mmm?

Client: It's not right, is it?

Therapist: How do you mean 'it'?

Client: People shouldn't talk to people like that, should they?

Therapist: But what about you, you don't like it, do you?

Client: Of course I don't, nobody would, would they?

Therapist: How is it for you, though?

Client: How do you think?

Therapist: I don't know, and I think it's hard to admit to another person, me, that 'I feel hurt.'

Client: Yes I think so. It is hard for me to be aware of what I feel and to talk about it, but I do feel quite cross about it.

Commentary

The client finds it hard to take ownership for his feelings of hurt and gains validity for his experience by attempting to normalize it. He externalizes the authority of his experience by appealing to the general as represented by the therapist rather than to the personal. The therapist remains focussed on that fundamental issue and invites the client to begin to reflect on his own situation and become aware of his own experience.

ILLUSTRATION

WORKING WITH AUTHENTICITY AND INAUTHENTICITY

Zack came to counselling complaining that he could not sleep and had out-bursts of anger at work. His line manager had suggested that he come. He said, 'It's just not like me … I want to get back to how I was, the real me. I was told you could give me some tips as a professional and tell me what the matter is. I've read that this sort of thing only takes a few sessions to sort out.' The counsellor replied, 'I don't think I'll be giving you any tips as such but I'm sure we can work together to find some.' Zack said, 'Oh, okay then, you're the expert.' The counsellor asked Zack to say something about his current life. He thought of himself as someone who helped other people, 'It's good to think of other people, isn't it?', he said. He stated that he had 'a pretty normal life, nothing special. It's just that people at work just keep doing such stupid things, deliberately to annoy me, like ….' He carried on with a story about other people's ways of doing things. Although it was not the sort of thing she usually did, the counsellor interrupted Zack to ask how he felt about a particular event. Zack said: 'Angry, I suppose, but anyone would, wouldn't they?' The counsellor said, 'Perhaps they would, I don't know, but I asked you how you felt, not how other people may have felt.' Zack could not see the difference.

He had recently changed jobs which meant he was now more self-directed. He agreed that it was a challenge but that he wanted to show his managers he could do it. 'They are really good people, they know their stuff.'

He was always a bit baffled by counselling and said that the latest problem was that his manager was encouraging him to come but his colleagues had found out and were critical of him. He said: 'What do you think? Do you think I should come?' His counsellor answered, 'Whether I want you to come or not is much less important than you being able to decide whether you want to come.' This led to an exploration of Zack's difficulty in knowing what he wanted and he finally began to see that he usually deferred to others' authority, giving up on his own.

Commentary

For a long time Zack had developed a number of ways (like pronoun switching and deferring to others) of avoiding having to know what he wanted, felt and needed. He had become an expert at finding out what others wanted and then would do exactly this. With his new job being self-directed this was beginning not to work any more and he was thrown back on his own authority only to find that he had little experience of using it or relying on it. It was crucial for him to have a therapist who could help him understand what had happened and how he might come into his own.

KEY POINTS

- Awareness of the irresolvable dilemmas of existence always evokes anxiety. Since anxiety can never be eliminated, our task is to find ways of living with it and perhaps even thriving on it.
- Authenticity is not just about being yourself or being real, it is about claiming authorship, taking responsibility for our actions and our life. It requires us to know life.
- Inauthenticity or self-deception is as much a part of living as authenticity since it is not possible to be constantly aware of all the factors of existence. Sometimes we just need to get on with things.

WORKING WITH DREAMS AND THE IMAGINATION

Existentially a dream is any product of the imagination. This can include a conventional dream we have when asleep, as well as a daydream, a fantasy, a story we make up, a picture we have painted, or a poem we have written or wish for the future. It can also include a story from a film or book that has significance for us.

Dreams are an integral part of our everyday life – they are the way we think and feel when we are asleep and they are just as important to us in relation to how we think and feel when we are awake. Just because they may not be so immediately understandable does not mean they can be disregarded – far from it.

They are an expression of the way we write our personal myth, about who we are, how we came to be and what we want to be. The dream images we use will be chosen for their evocative and emotional power rather than for their literal accuracy. This is the main reason the language is often different from everyday speech.

We will always inadvertently edit the dream in the telling and it is also all too easy to fall into the trap of interpreting and deciding what the dream 'really means' before really looking at it. Therapists too must resist this temptation, however obvious a meaning may seem. Like poems, dreams gain their power from having multiple resonances, from being both/and rather than either/or. In this way they are overdetermined. This means that there is no one correct – or two or three for that matter – meaning to a dream. But this does not mean that any meaning is as good as any other. The truth of a dream is decided by its resonance to the dreamer, and this will always be decided by the dreamer.

Existential issues are likely to be put more articulately in dreams and stories because they are ways we re-present our existence to ourselves. As such, they will include all the characteristic denials and evasions, paradoxes and dilemmas of our everyday life. They will also contain references to each of the four dimensions, the Physical – embodiment, the Social – kinship, the Personal – selfhood and the Spiritual – our overall worldview. The significance of the presence or absence of these is there to be understood.

Exploring dreams is done in the same way as exploring anything else the client brings – phenomenologically – and the therapist will encourage the dreamer to tell the dream as experienced without the logic and reactions of everyday thinking in order to reveal its significance. But because the meanings are often less immediately accessible, we need to take great care not to impose our meanings on the client.

We can systematically explore dreams in the following way. Do not lead, make your task the client's search for stronger engagement. Remember: it is the dreamer's dream, not yours. The dreamer must remain in charge of the process of unravelling. When the therapist takes over, they take over the client's autonomy. Also be aware that all conclusions are provisional and that meaning will be discovered by the dreamer. It may be that nothing seems to come of exploring a particular dream. It cannot be pushed and perhaps the meaning is not ready to be revealed until another time.

On the first telling of the dream, try not to seek clarification until the client has finished telling it:

> *Client:* I was in a car ... going on a long journey ... I don't know where ... with some other people, I didn't know them and it was getting quite hot in the car and the windows didn't open.

Then, rather than asking what the client thought it meant, ask them what it was like to tell the dream:

> *Client:* I don't know ... a bit uneasy ... uncomfortable.

Depending on what this reveals, then ask them to tell you the dream again but this time in the present tense. Ask for a complete, careful description with as much detail as possible, including descriptions of the background scene and atmosphere and also of any people or creatures present. It sometimes helps to ask the client to shut their eyes when re-telling:

> *Client:* I'm in a car ... I'm in the back seat ... I think it's my father's first car ... we're going away somewhere, on holiday I think ... it's going to take a long time ... there are three other people, my father's driving, I don't know the other two, I'm in the middle and they're talking to each other but I can't see them ... it's hot ... the windows won't open ... I can smell the hot leather and petrol ... I've got my hand on the door handle, I don't feel very well.

Again ask what it was like re-telling, and elicit what came up for them:

> *Client:* It was always like that when I was young ... holidays ... going somewhere I didn't know where or who with ... I wanted to be home with my friends and my mum ... even now, I don't like small spaces but I like staying at home, maybe that's why I never learnt to drive.

An alternative to the present tense can be telling the dream as a sequence of emotions rather than events, but still in the present tense:

Client: I'm anxious, a bit scared but also a bit excited, lonely, missing mum, annoyed with the other people who are enjoying themselves, sulky, isolated, having to pretend, frustrated, despairing, nothing I can do.

When you have done this, explore the dream systematically with the client. Don't interpret, but ask them what things in the dream remind them of and conjure up in terms of the four worlds. This has to be done carefully and the points below are not intended to be used like a questionnaire, merely as pointers.

Investigate the physical dimension:

- What is the material world that the dreamer is in: is it the natural, manmade or fantasy world?
- What are the laws observed, the material realities encountered?
- What are the objects, the animals, the creatures?
- What are the sensations experienced?
- Is the dreamer at ease in this physical world? Is it safe?
- Does the dreamer have control over movement and action? Is she active or passive? What is the experience of the dreamer's own body?
- Is there interaction with the bodies of others?

Client: Things are familiar but unusual … it took me right back to being 8 years old and holidays with my Dad and his new family. I didn't like them. I was just taken there and back, never really knew where or for how long. Trapped. I was too close to people I didn't know, I could smell them … it makes me want to hide in a corner.

Investigate the social dimension:

- What is the cultural context, the social context, the political context?
- Is the dreamer alone, or connected? Is he or she important or prominent? Anonymous or maybe just an observer?
- How many others are there? Are they close, familiar or distant and strange? Are they friendly or threatening, helpful or dangerous?
- Are they male, female, older, younger, similar or different to the dreamer?
- Is there co-operation, appreciation, community, or hostility and threat? Is there love, or aspiration to love?

Client: Who are these people? I don't know. Are they anything to do with me? They seem to be but I didn't know them, they are ignoring me, looked through me as if I'm not there. Lots of things I've got to do but I don't know why. Close, oppressive but untouchable and untouching … horrible. I hate it I don't like crowds or parties even.

Investigate the personal dimension:

- What is the personal world implied in the dream?
- Is the dreamer strong or weak? Confident or hesitant?

- Does he or she have a sense of identity and of recognition of this identity?
- Do they know what they want?
- What character traits are sketched out through the actions of the dream: courage or cowardice, intelligence or stupidity, self-reliance or need of others?
- What sort of a person is this person in the dream: what are his or her actions and motivations?
- What are his or her intentions and objectives?

Client: What do I want? Nothing. No, that's not right at all. I'm just there waiting for time to pass before I can get back home to my Mum ... you know, I saw a photo of a holiday I had at that time with my Dad and I was smiling, I must have enjoyed myself, I suppose, but it didn't feel like it ... I wanted him to think I was, I really did ... but I couldn't show it ... he always seemed pleased to see me but ... I feel so bad now he's dead and I can't tell him how much I loved him.

Investigate the spiritual world:

- What is the worldview expressed in this dream?
- What sort of world does the dreamer believe he or she lives in?
- What are the values expressed?
- What kind of morality is displayed?
- What is it that makes the dream meaningful?
- What are the expressed wishes and desires?
- What is it that really matters at the end of the day and what stands in the way of achieving it?

Client: People are OK, I suppose, they don't bother me if I don't bother them. I know how I'm supposed to be. I can't ask for much, I've got no room to move, but they are not going to hurt me, just ignore me, it's fixed, they've decided. No choice.

Think about the following:

- What is the relationship between the dreamer and the dream?
- Is the dreamer in the dream, or looking at themselves in the dream?
- What is the dreamer's attitude to the dream?
- What is the dreamer's attitude to dreaming?
- In what way is the therapist–client relationship referred to in the dream?
- Can the dream be thought of as one in a sequence?

When you have carefully explored all these dimensions, ask the dreamer how all this applies to their everyday experience. It is at this point that you can wonder about the elements that have been missed out.

- What has the dreamer learnt about his or her own style, mode of being in the world?
- What has he or she learnt about her own attitude and actions and their possible consequences?

- What lessons are there here for the future?
- What are the paradoxes and dilemmas in the dream?
- What changes might be required in everyday life in order to accommodate the teaching of the dream?
- What is the existential message?

Client: It's like everything, isn't it? I'm a player in somebody else's plan. You asked about the door handle – that I can get out but I don't. I want to go but I want to stay as well, like with Jim, my boyfriend. People are perfectly nice but I want them to make the first move, silly, isn't it? How would it be different if I got out or if I talked to them? Risky, they may not want to talk to me, but they don't anyway and it's me that's making it happen that way. The fear's worse than the thing, and it's not getting me what I want. It's like what we were talking about last week, isn't it? I expect you to ask me questions and then I don't answer them.

KEY POINTS

- A dream is anything which is the product of the imagination.
- Dreams have multiple meanings.
- The client is the ultimate judge of the meaning of a dream.
- Dreams must be explored phenomenologically.
- The meanings of a dream will be revealed through careful description.

6

WHAT REALLY MATTERS TO THE CLIENT

If real success is to attend the effort to bring a man to a definite position, one must first of all take pains to find HIM where he is and begin there. This is the secret of the art of helping others.

Søren Kierkegaard

SOME FIRST PRINCIPLES

The majority of clients have little interest in how psychotherapy works. They just want help in living a better life. They have reached a point in their lives where they do not want things to continue as they are, but do not know how to change them. They simply want to get on with their lives and not get into their usual traps and dead ends. Some clients hope for a painless solution – symptom relief. This puts the existential therapist in something of a dilemma because we see symptoms, i.e. depression, phobias, addictions and anxiety not as relatively meaningless events to be removed by magic words or medication, but as indicators that the way the person is living their life is unsatisfactory to them – they are the ontic (everyday) correlates of ontological (being related) anxiety.

The ways we evade and deny reality often form the basis of symptoms. Beneath every symptom is an unfaced dilemma. Essentially clients come to therapy when their usual evasions and denials are not working as well as they used to and they need a new way of tackling the problem, but feel at a loss to find one.

So we need to find a way to take our clients' concerns and their desire for relief seriously while at the same time promoting an open curiosity about the challenges of existence. This is not always easy. Many clients will have struggled with their questions for some time and maybe only found temporary relief. Which is why they have turned to therapy. Even those clients on medication know at some level that they will have to manage without it sometime. Neither of us, in the many settings we have worked in over several decades have ever met one client who was happy to stay on medication indefinitely, though some felt they had to. They know that the issues that brought them to therapy will remain unchanged unless they look at them, engage with them and try to change them. They know that medication only buys them some time of symptom relief. This can sometimes be a good and necessary thing. But there are drawbacks to it and many complain that medication ultimately makes things harder rather than easier.

So although clients want immediate relief, they also are aware that they are unlikely to get it and that in order to get better, they will need to put in some really hard work, facing up to their problems and difficulties.

Clients who wish for symptom relief and treat the therapist like an expert who is there to tell them what to do or how to think are best advised from the outset that existential therapy may not be their best bet. It is very difficult if not impossible to do existential work with a client who is not ready to ask questions about the human condition in general and their own way of living life in particular. Sometimes people grow into this new way of tackling their problems after initial reluctance and scepticism.

In general, clients wish:

- to be understood and to feel that if they keep working at it they will ultimately understand themselves a bit better;
- to be supported in their tentative steps into the unknown;
- to feel they are not the only person to feel as they do and to be released of shame about not coping as well as they feel they ought to.

They are unlikely to know these things by simply being told that they are so or by being reassured. They will need to discover all these strange and amazing things by themselves, with our help, so that they can experience and understand them. Existential therapy is a process of uncovering and discovery.

DILEMMAS, CONFLICTS AND TENSIONS

In existential therapy, the client's question is evidence of a keenly felt human dilemma that needs exploring. Many issues are experienced and reported as simple polarized opposites when they are in fact complex and have many facets. Although polarizing is an attempt to simplify, it actually makes the issue more intractable because it excludes some aspects of the dilemma which have to be included for it to be understood. The either/or solution always involves trying to have one set of feelings or thoughts instead of another set. In these cases we need to take the person back a step or two to reconsider the issue from all sides. We may say things like:

- Hang on a minute there, let's not jump to conclusions.
- Perhaps we need to backtrack a bit and consider things more carefully.
- You are assuming quite a lot here, let's pause and look at this again.

Sometimes it is difficult for people to make a decision because they are reluctant to take the responsibility of letting go of something they thought essential. They wish to hang on to the illusion of not having to give anything up and erroneously assume they can avoid anxiety by not choosing or by getting someone else or circumstances to make the decision for them. Therapists have to be able to recognize such hesitations for what they are and gently encourage further explorations.

Initially, in their search for quick and clear answers that will cure all their ills, clients are inclined to ask direct questions of their therapist. They will ask: 'What should I do?' or 'You're the expert, so what's the answer to my problem?' Many therapists learn in their training that such questions should not be answered and that they should instead observe what can often be an awkward silence, or simply reflect the question back to the client or interpret that they are making themselves dependent on the assumed wisdom of the therapist. All these will rightfully enrage or disappoint the client, and especially so early on in therapy. Therapists may falsely assume that the client is easily able to reflect for themselves. Sometimes this is so, but more often than not the client is exasperated by having tried it themselves without success. None of these interventions are wrong when said at the right time, and as said before, silence can often be a very powerful and fertile prompt, but they are inappropriate when the client feels stuck or desperate because they deny the client the help they need in finding direction. They can be felt as persecutory or abandoning.

A more existential way to respond to such a question is to encourage the client to consider their predicament in a new way and reply by saying: 'What is it like not to know what to do and not to know what the answer is?' And the client may reply something like: 'Pretty awful, actually, but I would really like you to tell me what the answer is.' And at this point we can ask the client to consider whether this is truly what they wish for or whether they have come to learn for themselves how to find their own way around their problems.

Most people know that when lost they are better off with a map so that they can find their own way, rather than remaining blindfolded while someone leads them out passively to safety (or into an impasse). Most of us value our autonomy and a sense of purpose. But it is also important to have a clear idea of our destination, rather than just being told where to go. Therapists initially need to help their clients articulate their sense of direction, destination and aspirations.

In this we need to be direct and fair, while having faith in our clients' ability for reflection, understanding and action. This means tackling problems and dilemmas head on, while showing how this can be done most steadily by going slowly, step by step.

It is often valuable to start by agreeing with the client what the precise problem is and to reformulate it as a dilemma so that its various contradictory elements can be explored. In this process we ask them to describe the sensations, feelings, thoughts and intuitions they have without trying to justify, explain or put them into good order. This is not as easy as it sounds because it is difficult to experience opposite feelings at the same time. But it will eventually bring all facets of the dilemma into view.

- One of the most effective existential interventions is to paraphrase the experience of having the dilemma, as in: 'So, on the one hand, you feel angry/disappointed/ triumphant, but, on the other hand, you also feel sad/relieved/guilty.' This is often followed up with: 'What does that tension feel like?'

Often dilemmas can only be overcome effectively by transcending them: this means including some aspects of each side of the dilemma into our final choice of a solution by thinking dialectically. Let's assume, for instance, that someone is torn between staying in a job that provides them with much safety and a steady routine but in which they do not feel challenged, and taking on an offer of being part of a risky adventure which might lead to a new career and self-development but where they may regret what they have given up and where they fear it might all go wrong. The clear way ahead is to find a third option, in which they can steadily build a new career without taking the huge risk of burning all their bridges.

Of course, there are many ways to resolve dilemmas and this is a part of the problem. Resolving a dilemma involves truthfully knowing one's desires, strengths and weaknesses and committing to a choice. In the process of working this out, life becomes much more fluid and far more promising than it ever was before.

The final solution is not an either/or, and might involve neither of the two options that brought the dilemma to light. It transcends the original issues.

Looking our difficulties in the eye may be hard, but it is also the beginning of improvement and transformation. Therapists need to have a sense of determination, courage, confidence and also of humour and empathy with the client's plight, if they are to free up the client's reluctance to start doing the hard work.

KEY POINTS

- Symptoms are created by avoidance of dilemmas and by denial and disengagement.
- Clients need to be helped to become first of all aware of the contradictions they are dealing with and this almost always means increasing their awareness of the tension.
- Clients may initially evade this tension and often have spent many years refining their own personal ways of pretending it does not exist.
- Awareness of tension first happens through facing the contradictory emotions we experience. Anxiety, guilt, despair, shame, anger and disappointment are the harbingers of hidden dilemmas.

THE PHYSICAL DIMENSION.
COMING FACE TO FACE WITH
LIFE AND DEATH: THE REALITY
OF CHANGE AND LOSS IN THE *UMWELT*

Of all the dilemmas and tensions that we have to contend with, the tension between life and death is the most fundamental. None of us can avoid the remarkable irony that we are all born to die. Ultimately everything is temporary. Our desire to note important life events is evidence of this. Our birthday or the date we originated is celebrated, as is each new year, the first day at school because they are each symbolic of a new beginning. We value other milestones too: the first separation from our parents, our first secret, our first sexual experience, parenthood, mid-life, or the death of someone close to us all remind us of the reality of change and loss.

In fact, every passing moment reminds us our time is getting shorter, although we often do not discover this until there are few moments left to enjoy.

EXERCISE

Imagine your life as an hour glass where sand runs through the narrowing from the top to the bottom. You can see the amount of sand in the lower bulb, but the upper bulb is covered up so you cannot see it. How much sand do you think is in the upper bulb? Now uncover the upper bulb. What do you see? What do you feel?

Paradox and dilemma

The paradox of the physical world is that life only teaches us how to survive, but death teaches us how to live. Life is a taskmaster, while death is a master teacher. The unsolvable dilemma is that mortality is a constant fact of our lives which we can either welcome, accept, deny or fear.

When a client first faces the fact that: 'My life is mine and nobody else's and it will end soon', they realize paradoxically both their difference from and also their similarity to other people. We all die alone – yet we all share the fact of this reality. We do not engage with this dilemma easily and rarely by choice. It is mainly when we are forced to – when things go wrong.

So, the basic question we address in this dimension is: 'How can I live my life fully while knowing I may die at any moment?'

We often deny this by:

- being 'logical' about it or pretending it does not matter;
- imagining death as a peaceful and restful sleep, rather than as the absence of being;
- believing in an after-life, or by leaving a memorial of some sort;

- believing in an 'ultimate rescuer' – God, a parent, a doctor, or even a therapist – a tendency for dependency on others;
- being depressed, helpless and withdrawn;
- pursuing youthfulness;
- by opting out of life before it can opt out on us, i.e. by attempting or committing suicide.

All the above strategies may bring some temporary relief, but they ultimately do more harm than good. Rigid and protective strategies require constant shoring up in the face of reality, with the result that the individual's existential anxieties take on an increasingly extreme and dysfunctional form.

ILLUSTRATION

WORKING WITH THE PHYSICAL DIMENSION

Adrian had run marathons for many years. He had been proudly working towards becoming part of the 100 club: a group of people who had run 100 marathons. He spent most of his time training and preparing for the next feat. His family life was by now almost non-existent, since his wife objected greatly to his obsessive behaviour and resented him spending so little time at home. Eventually, on the eve of one of his most important runs, she set him a huge dilemma and challenged him to 'choose for your running or for me'. He could not solve this dilemma and went to his marathon with heavy heart. He collapsed in the race and had to be taken into hospital, with heart problems. He had no idea how this had happened and felt his wife had thrown a spell over him. He came to counselling only because he was so puzzled about how this was possible.

Commentary

It took quite some time before Adrian was able and willing to question himself and to understand the profound meaning of what had happened. After a while of talking about his preoccupations and worries he began to realize there was a paradox underneath his predicament. He had been so busy proving his fitness and immortality that he had lost track of everything else in his life, including, ironically, his own health and his relationship: the two things that it was worth caring for. Now that he had seen the possibility of death, he could think of it in a different way. He decided to be less excessive in his pursuit of fitness and let go of the idea of the 100 club. Ultimately he found a way to include his wife in his sport and they began exercising together, trying out a variety of options and finally settling on sailing. But what really made the difference for Adrian was that he had been able to let go of his obsession with beating others and beating life and that he felt he had finally come to himself. Adrian's fear of death which led him to devote himself to running and which nearly killed him, was actually based on his fear of his unlived life. Confronting his fear of death enabled him to live his life.

KEY POINTS

- Because it is so hard for a client to talk about death, it is important the therapist acknowledges and respects the client's defences, as well as being willing and able to challenge them.
- Since it is so difficult to engage with death, extremely strong reactions are likely, there may be suicidal thoughts, a return to addictions or other damaging behaviour, or wishing to end the therapy.
- It may not just be the client who is unwilling to talk about death, the therapist may also be unwilling. Not only does a therapist need to know about their own death and related issues, they need to be open enough to hear the client's emerging thoughts and feelings without imposing theirs.
- Since existence is composed of life and death, talking about death too much in therapy can be a way of evading the responsibilities and the possibilities of the brightness of life.
- Since loss may be easier to talk about, a client may talk about it instead of bringing up the more difficult topic of death.
- We need to be alert to the client's references to mortality and regrets about what they have been able or not been able to achieve in their life. References to birthdays and anniversaries are worth noting in this respect.

THE SOCIAL DIMENSION. ISOLATION AND CONNECTEDNESS: RELATIONSHIPS IN THE *MITWELT*

No matter what clients first bring to therapy, difficulties with relationships will invariably emerge over the ensuing weeks and months. Adrian's problem, for instance, was at least as much about his relationship with his wife as it was about his consuming desire to be fit and athletic and overcome his emerging physical limitations.

Relationship patterns are often based on the sedimented assumptions we made about relationships when we were most impressionable, in our childhood and teenage years. Consequently we get used to expecting certain qualities in our relationships and find it difficult to see any alternative. Most of the time it works well enough but a client may come to psychotherapy when either the client or someone in their circle changes their priorities.

Different layers of social relationship

Some relationships are more anonymous: they range from our chance meetings with strangers to the formalized relationships we have with bureaucracy. Others are more personal: these are with the people we get to know as individuals in our social and work networks. Then there are those with people we really open up to. These are reserved for the people we love and are included in the personal world that will be discussed later. The distinguishing factor between all these is the extent to which we are prepared to share intimate details and secrets with others.

A paradox of therapy is that it takes place in all three of these areas at the same time and this is why it is so hard and so necessary to maintain appropriate boundaries.

In common with other technology-based cultures, our society not only idealizes personal independence but also tends to technologize relationships by leading people to believe that there are simple tricks and gimmicks that can be learnt to make them better. Thinking of sexual relationships in terms of sexual technique and prowess rather than in terms of interpersonal intimacy is a good example of this. Co-creating good relationships, for it is never a purely individual task, is an art that takes a lifetime to perfect.

Paradox and dilemma

The paradox of the social world is that it is only by awareness of our separateness from others that we are able to get close because it allows us to learn to understand them – and ourselves. As long as we treat others as if they are the same as us, or should be, we will be disappointed.

The unsolvable dilemma is that we want to bridge our distance from others and fuse with them, while simultaneously needing to establish our separateness and our individuality.

The foundation of all relationships is the need to belong, to be acknowledged, appreciated and valued. But it is also the need to be able to love, appreciate, acknowledge and value in return.

Existentially, the right sorts of relationships are characterized by mature interdependence with others, not by either dependency on or independence from others. We need other people to appreciate us but we also need to have our separateness and difference appreciated. We find it hard to face up to the utter strangeness and mystery of love: of what it means to be loved or not loved, to be wanted or to be left alone.

The basic question clients address in this dimension is: 'What are other people there for?'

We often deny this by:

- avoiding intimate relationships altogether, preferring to keep relationships on an acquaintance level;
- finding many excuses to not spend time alone, talking or just being with the other;
- seeing relationships as competitive, with winners and losers;
- mistaking challenging for fighting, and lust for intimacy and infatuation for love;
- reducing our social world to the bare minimum we need to survive.

Clients want:

- to manage their relationships better;
- to appreciate others and be appreciated by others;
- to understand how relationships work and what their part in them is;
- to understand why they keep on having particular sorts of relationships and mess them up over and over again.

EXERCISE

Think of five people in your life. Take a sheet of paper and draw a circle and write their names equidistantly on the outside of the circle. Put yourself in the centre of the circle. Draw a line between yourself and all the people on the outside of the circle like spokes in a wheel. Think about the relationship you have with them in terms of support, sharing and disclosure.

Taking each relationship in turn, think about how much you feel supported by the other or support the other. If you feel you support the other a lot put three arrows going from you to that person, a moderate amount – two arrows, a little – one arrow. Similarly, draw inward pointing arrows for how much you feel you are supported by them. You will end up with a chart that tells you how much support is going out from your circle and how much is coming in.

- Are the amounts equal?
- What does this tell you about the kind of relationships you have?
- What are the different sorts of support in your life? Are they enough?
- What are the strengths and limitations of each relationship?
- How would you like it to change?
- What are the obstacles to change?
- What does that feel like?

If you have an opportunity to discuss your observations with the people in question, find out whether their perception is the same as yours. Often we emphasize the support we give and we may even resent it, while being unaware of the support we receive in turn but take for granted.

One issue revealed by this exercise is that the way we find ourselves in a world with others varies from moment to moment and from person to person.

With respect to our clients we need to know:

- Are there many people in their life or only a few?
- Are they dominant or submissive in relation to these others?
- Are they competitive or cooperative, active or passive, engaged or withdrawn, trusting or suspicious?

Trust and control

Existential therapy is a relationship which is founded on trust and the value of understanding, but in order to be understood, we have to be known and therefore we have to risk showing our weaknesses and shortcomings. The overall aim of therapy will be to discover the experience of liberation rather than the experience of constraint and threat, that intimacy can bring. But in order that the intimacy can be gained, its future loss must be risked, for true intimacy cannot be controlled or forced. Both people must be able to make a free choice to be with the other.

More often than not it is the process of the therapy rather than its content that will reflect the trust. Clients are more likely to believe our respect when we respect our own authority as much as theirs. If this means that we challenge them on how they treat us, then this is a natural part of cooperation and respect. Progress will be measured at least as much by an increase in cooperation and trust between the therapist and client as by what the client says they do outside therapy.

Competitiveness and objectification

Both Martin Buber and Jean-Paul Sartre said that we reduce people's unpredictability by making them into objects, by making them into an 'It'. But in doing so we make ourselves into objects too. We think it will make things simpler and it does, but at a cost. It leads us to attribute human qualities to objects, material qualities to humans and causation to interpersonal relationships.

Sartre's trilogy 'The Roads to Freedom' vividly describes how the various characters see themselves not as dynamically co-constituted in-the-world, but rather as objects who are caused by the world, but are unable to see their way out.

It helps to remember that most relationship problems rest on the fears of losing both our individuality and the love of the other. This comes out by taking on the roles of victim, persecutor or rescuer in the relationship. Of the three, the victim role is often seen as the favoured position, to feel most 'done to' – to have the least agency:

- The person in the victim role feels and presents themselves as 'done to' by the other and as powerless to stand up to them. While there is a possibility that in yielding, a tension may be overcome or that the other may be made aware of their own impact, usually it leads to defeatism and despair.
- The person in the persecutor role seeks to cajole or control the other so that they do things 'properly'. It may help us to feel good about our ability to move things forward, but since we do it for our own benefit, the other person is actually diminished and feels bullied.
- The person in the rescuer role looks for other people to help and they make saving the other person their project. While we can feel good about our own capacity for care, since we rescue for our own benefit, the other person is prevented from finding their own dignity and independence. It depletes them and takes away their autonomy.

These roles are taken up in co-dependent relationships where although a person may wish for the other to change in some way – which is why they act as they do – in fact if one of the couple changed it would destabilize the relationship and risk something new happening. Addiction is often a strong component in co-dependent relationships.

The word 'role' is used to indicate that it is a position we take up in order to protect our vulnerability. Although superficially different, what all three roles have in common is that they all deny personal responsibility and objectify themselves and others rather than acknowledging the difficulty of trust.

EXERCISE

- Which of the positions of victim, persecutor and rescuer do you find yourself in most frequently?
- In everyday life, as a therapist and as a client?
- And second most frequently?
- What are your gains and losses of being in it?
- What do you do to get out?

The therapy situation can easily replicate the rescuer–victim relationship with the therapist as the rescuer and the client as the victim to be rescued. It takes a lot of training and experience to recognize such patterns and also to use this recognition to good effect.

ILLUSTRATION

WORKING WITH THE SOCIAL DIMENSION

Mike, a 27-year-old man, came to therapy after the break-up of a two-year relationship with Marie. He found it hard to say why they had decided to finish except that they were making each other unhappy. He did not understand what went wrong except that they had become very critical of each other whereas they used to support each other. They had stopped fancying each other.

He talked about how lonely he was. At one point during this phase his therapist suggested some ways to meet more people and he missed the next session. Fortunately she realized that his absence was related to her advice and this led to an understanding of his protective self-sufficiency and how he felt people were trying to control him by telling him what to do but also that he felt scared of the therapist's attack if he said so. All he wanted was for his therapist to listen to him. This was quite challenging enough because he was not used to sharing his thoughts and feelings with another person. He also did not understand why he and his partner cared about each other now that they were apart whereas when they were together they did not. Although he wanted to be back with her, she did not. He thought he could get her back by being understanding.

After some time trying to understand why just being close to someone could bring up such confusing feelings he met someone else, 'fell in love'. He was sure that it would work this time. His therapist was not so sure and said so but he took no notice and gave up his job and therapy and moved to Spain to be with her. After

(Continued)

(Continued)

six months he came back as the relationship had not worked out at least in part because he had slept with one of her best friends. This in fact had been a pattern of his. The work resumed. He had frequently come a few minutes late for every session. This had been referred to but had been met with excuses of traffic, alarm clock or work problems. The therapist felt that although Mike seemed to work hard in therapy when he was there, she never felt that he took much notice of her or what she said. This was put to him and it revealed a connection he had between trust and control, '… either I can be myself on my own, or I lose myself with some-one else … what am I supposed to do?' He realized that by coming late he retained some control over the therapy by reducing the time he had. Short-changing himself seemed a small price to pay to maintain control. But he did not want to pay that price any more. This marked the beginning of the next phase of therapy where he came on time. The relationship with his therapist was beginning to matter. He allowed himself to talk about his anxiety about breaks and holidays. He was in dialogue. Also during this time he decided that sexual relationships were just too problematic and he gave them up until he knew what he wanted from others. He later met someone and this time it was different, 'I used to think that closeness to another person meant I had to give things up, that we had to think the same, but we don't and it doesn't matter and what's more I still fancy her, I feel closer but also freer than I've felt before. I was always looking for the right one before, but it's not about that at all, it's about my ability to commit to a choice.'

Commentary

Prior to therapy, Mike's relationships were either short, with little emotional involvement or had a strong but dependent quality in which he and the woman needed each other for mutual support. He moved between too much distance and too much closeness which usually degenerated into blame. In therapy he was able to experience what it meant to be listened to and discovered that trust could be freeing and not constraining and conditional. His way of relating to others paralleled his way of relating in therapy and the combination of talking about his issues of intimacy went hand in hand with experiencing his therapist in a different non-abandoning and non-intrusive way. This in turn led to his being able to experience others in this way. For the first time he was able to make a choice and commit himself to his choice.

KEY POINTS

- Relationships are unavoidable, but risky as well as satisfying. Most people want more fulfilling relationships but they are doubtful about the risks this brings.
- In the search for new ways of being with others, a client may fall back on earlier ways of justifying their self-destructive behaviour.

- Paradoxically, the motivation to form and maintain close relationships is not only heightened by an awareness of death, but such relationships also enable us to tolerate the terror of death.
- It is important to get a measure of the quality of the client's intimate relationships. A pointer to this is by asking the client, 'What would your partner/mother think about what you are saying to me if they were in the room with us now?'
- Not everyone ends up in a position of social isolation by choice. People whose opportunity for social contact is limited through unemployment, shift work or through a commitment as a full-time carer can be susceptible simply by circumstance to a reduced social world. In those cases renewed opportunities for social connection might straighten out the situation fairly quickly without further therapeutic intervention.
- Sometimes meeting with a therapist will be the only meaningful social contact client gets and for this reason they will be reluctant to finish therapy. This must be addressed so that the client increases their social circle in other ways.
- It is often helpful to provide a group therapy experience for people in this situation either in addition to therapy, or after it has finished.
- It is rarely possible to talk about relationship issues without the issues being present and worked on in the relationship between therapist and client.
- People keep repeating old patterns of relating until they have understood where they go wrong. The term 'working through' is useful because it reminds us to beware of quick solutions and to make sure that people really grasp the way in which they relate.

THE PERSONAL DIMENSION. FREEDOM AND A PERSONAL SENSE OF INTEGRITY: LIFE PATTERNS AND THE ORIGINAL PROJECT IN THE *EIGENWELT*

One of the landmarks in the work with Mike was when he saw his repeating sequence of denying his needs, finding flaws with others, moving away from them and then looking for someone else, only to discover that they too were not right. He came to realize that the common factor in all his relationships was himself and that his pattern was a way to avoid his relational nature by repeating what was familiar. This marked the beginning of being able to think about his life and to take responsibility for it, to realize that rather than being created by it, he created it himself. This realization allowed him to have choice over a situation he previously thought was automatic. He became active rather than passive, and the passivity which led to weakness and confusion was due to his denial of personal responsibility.

The personal world is concerned with issues of responsibility, choice, freedom and personal integrity. It acknowledges a world of personal thoughts that is mine and no one else's. Awareness of this sense of 'mineness' evokes anxiety, since it makes us not only responsible for our own experiences and aware that others are responsible for theirs, but also that we are connected, that my sense of who I am is derived from my relationships with others. When this happens, it becomes possible perhaps for the first time to see our lives as chosen but also as random and this may make us anxious.

We may seek to quell this anxiety by various means, taking the easy life, until we discover that taking personal responsibility for making up our own mind is the only way forward if we want to become truly awake and in charge of our life.

Original project

We have an overriding need to make sense of ourselves and the world we are in and we do this in different ways depending on our age and our knowledge. Sartre says that this leads us to choose an 'original project' of how to be. It is always a reactive, emotionally based and age-appropriate unspoken choice that the child makes about the best way to preserve their autonomy. But it is always a choice. It is us who give events their meaning by our choices. For example, someone who was ill treated when young may grow up to see themselves as a victim. Or they may think of themselves as a survivor. Neither is determined. Both are choices. There are clearly contextual constraints but what is important is the extent to which the event or quality is used by the person as a restricting act of self-definition so that it becomes a self-fulfilling prophecy. This is how our original project shapes our lives and becomes sedimented as our sense of self. Because of the emotional stakes involved, an original project is rarely negotiable at the time and it is only when it becomes well past its 'sell-by' date and starts to cause problems that people may realize it exists. This often coincides with a person's decision to come to therapy.

Existentially the past, present and future are equally important. The present holds the possibility of breaking free of past decisions and of facing the future with courage but only if choices made in the past are understood and owned.

If a client does not understand the meaning of the present, they will be repeating the past. It is by having it pointed out by the therapist and by observing their own denial and noting its consequences that the client can find out how they evaded responsibility in the past. And as they puzzle over the new meaning of the past and see how their choices impacted on their world, they begin to get an inkling of how they currently limit their own lives and start wondering whether they might change this for the future. This breaking free of past choices and deliberately making new choices and commitments is often felt like an existential birth. It is about understanding the law of consequences and the person's place in it. It is being able to say: 'I did this, I made this choice, and as a consequence I felt that and I can take responsibility for the consequences of my choices and actions.'

Where previously a person reacted to existing rules with either passive agreement or automatic rejection, they can now consider which course of action to own and take personal responsibility for. It may well be that what is chosen is similar to what others have chosen. This is not important. The point is that it be owned.

Paradox and dilemma

The paradox of the personal world is therefore that when we realize we are vulnerable, we find our strength. When we discover that there is no external rule book, the freedom that follows allows us to discover responsibility and the possibility of choice.

The unsolvable dilemma is that while we search for some principles that apply universally, we have to own the authority of our own experience while keeping other people and the rest of the world in view. We have no option but to act as if we know where we are going until experience proves us right or wrong.

The basic question clients address in this dimension is: 'How can I be me?' Associated with this is another question which directs them towards the past, 'How did I become the person I am?', and also one that looks to the future 'Will I be able to stop making the same mistakes and live more resourcefully in the future?'

Personal world work is demanding on the therapist because the dilemmas will often be denied by:

- excessive assertion of individuality and the uniqueness of ideas and actions;
- assertion of powerlessness or lack of agency;
- avoiding being alone so as to not have to face the anxiety of thinking about our own world and the choices and responsibilities it holds;
- being alone and withdrawing from the world in solitude, refusing to engage out of fear;
- excessively deferring to others for an opinion or judgement, including the therapist;
- systematic rejection of others' viewpoints, including the therapist's;
- using TV, food, alcohol, newspapers, internet, activity, sex, shopping, gambling, i.e. the 'addictions' to tranquillize ourselves, thereby subverting the therapy;
- maintaining that either we have achieved everything in life or that we are unable to achieve anything in life.

ILLUSTRATION

WORKING WITH THE PERSONAL DIMENSION

Sophie first contacted her therapist by email, saying: 'I am currently in a confused, destructive space and hope to find an environment in which to learn more about myself.' She was 23 years old and worked in the popular music industry and was in an on–off relationship with Alan who was 10 years older, who while he was very interested in her, also told her how she should conduct her life. She was drawn to him though she did not think the relationship was safe and was reluctant to open up to him. She had given up on expecting the relationship to be equal. She had been experiencing a recurrence of bulimia, was drinking too much and was fighting a desire to cut herself. She knew this just wasn't right but didn't know how to deal with the overwhelming feelings.

(Continued)

(Continued)

She had not confided in anyone else about these problems since she found it hard to talk about herself, even in therapy. She was more used to listening than talking. She wept for almost the whole of the first session, apologizing. Her therapist just listened. She knew immediately that this was what was so special about the relationship – Alan was the first person she could remember who had been interested in what she thought and felt. She talked about when she was growing up, and when her two older brothers would play together and exclude her, while her parents argued. She found solace from a young age in going for long walks in the woods nearby where they lived and had found a dark hollow in which she could sit and hide. It was still easy for her to go for days on end without seeing anyone. She wanted to leave her job because she had begun to realize that she had no interest in it and did not like the relationships she had there with lots of 'self-absorbed, narcissistic people' who she had to pander to. They were like her family – 'high maintenance'. She took pride in the fact that she was not. In therapy she slowly became aware of experiencing other people as a threat to herself. She had dreams of being hounded by dragons and other monsters. And while her response initially was to turn away and hide, feeling weak in herself, through the therapy she began to see the courage and strength she had in order to define herself as capable of tending to others and staying separate instead of being destroyed by their demands and conflicts. What she had never done, however, was to express any of this. Her frustrations were kept inside of her body, which she then treated as badly as other people treated her.

Commentary

Sophie had to begin to affirm herself as a person of worth and a person with strength, but also as a person who had rights in relation to others. Instead of feeling guilty in her rather odd relationship to Alan, she began to see that his interest in her was an opportunity to find out who she really was in relation to others. But also that it was restricting in rather familiar ways. She began to formulate her needs and desires and started practising expressing her own thoughts to other people as well as letting them know when she didn't want to talk to them. Her struggle was one of finding her own strength as well as accepting her own needs and desires in relation to others. As this capacity to affirm herself improved, so her symptoms slowly became redundant.

KEY POINTS

- The following interventions may be useful when thinking about the personal world and the original project:
- 'Is there anything familiar about what happened then and what is happening now?'
- 'What's it like when you find yourself making the same mistake?'

- 'What do you think led up to this conclusion?'
- 'What was your part in that sequence of events?'
- 'What's it like that you now discover that you were covering up the truth from yourself?'
- 'How did your action lead to that unexpected conclusion?'
- 'How is what you are doing going to lead you to what you want?'
- Although clients may initially deny their willingness to get to know themselves, let alone love or value themselves, this is a measure of how hard they have found it in the past.
- In order to make a new and free rather than a reactive choice we need to go back to the feeling that we had when deciding on the original project and re-examine the choice.
- Clients can easily become curious about the therapist's ideas about life. Our value to clients is not so much in terms of the rules we have discovered, it is that we know what it is like to realize that there are none and what it means to work them out for ourselves and own them. Therapists should beware when clients agree with everything the therapist says just as much as when they disagree with everything.
- As we become more familiar with the personal dimension, we learn to appreciate what we value about ourselves and understand and forgive what we find problematic or difficult. And this stance will inevitably be applied to others.
- The prototype dysfunction in the personal dimension is to take responsibility for things one does not have responsibility for and to deny responsibility for those things one does have responsibility for.
- Therapists may need to help clients to formulate strengths and weaknesses and help in making the most of both.
- Finding a sense of direction that can be affirmed for the good of those around us as well as for ourselves is not a bad aim for therapy.
- To be flexible in our experience of ourselves as we change and mature over the years and kind to ourselves in our fallibility and limitations is another worthwhile aim for therapy.
- Existentially, human development is largely the consequence of how we engage with chance and opportunity in the context of uncertainty.

THE SPIRITUAL DIMENSION. CONSISTENCY OF VALUES, BELIEFS AND PRINCIPLES IN THE *ÜBERWELT*

Sophie's problems were focused on the way she experienced herself in relation to other people and this meant that she could only change if she dared to take up more space in the world. Without realizing it, she had learnt to live her life in terms of other people's desires, needs and expectations. She was very good at this, but was paying the price of feeling like a shadow rather than a real person. Stuffing herself with food and injuring herself were ways of experimenting with self-enlargement and self-intensification without bothering other people with her needs and her presence.

Beneath her unspoken and initially unknown assumptions were a myriad of values and beliefs that blocked her and stifled her capacity for change. One of these beliefs was that people should be considerate of each other and deep down she believed that inconsiderate and demanding people like her family and work colleagues were bad and that she was good for being self-effacing. This was one of her core values. But she was also unable to admit that she longed for someone to pay attention to her and put her needs first, for a change. Her relationship with Alan initially appeared to offer this, but did not come about because his view of her coincided with her own view of herself – as someone without needs. This confused her greatly because she saw Alan as good for giving her attention but also bad for often disappointing her. And she concluded that she rather than him must be doing something wrong.

As she became more self-reflective about herself in human relationships she began to see that who she thought she was might not be who she really was. Her self-image had been based on a wrong and partial view.

None of this would have been possible if her therapist had not given her space to take some perspective on herself and ask herself some new questions about the meaning of her life.

The *Überwelt* refers to the world above, or to put it another way, the ability to see the world from a bird's eye view, from above. This is how we learn to make sense of things. And find meaning in life. As long as we remain engaged exclusively with the bodily, interpersonal and intrapersonal realities, we find it hard to have this sort of perspective.

Faith, crisis and trauma

Even the most rational person's assumptions about the world and its future are based on faith rather than fact, on probability and hope rather than certainty. Faith in science is about the predictability and linearity of the universe, and faith in religion is about the existence of a god and specific rules for living. Existentially, faith is about the commitment to make sense of our existence even though we may never fully understand what it is for or how best to conduct it. We cannot help but fall back on belief in predictability and coherence as a necessary ontological delusion that enables us to achieve our ambitions. Even suicide involves a faith that we will not be punished for our actions and that it is better to be dead than alive. Since we cannot know for certain if this is true, this is a gamble, to say the least. Nevertheless, life is predictable much of the time, but whenever it stops being so our value-laden universe unravels and we lose the capacity to be purposeful. Existentially we are traumatized by randomness, chance and unexpected malice. These are a reminder that our place in the universe is uncertain and ephemeral.

Whether such trauma is sudden or cumulative, it cannot be easily integrated, so we shut down instead or resort to self-blame and flounder in hopelessness.

But such unravelling contains within it the possibility of taking a broader view of existence and of reconsidering some of our previously strongly held beliefs that have been shown to be faulty or incomplete. Moments of crisis, trauma and catastrophe have this redeeming feature of allowing us to review and rebuild our lives. It is therefore hugely important that we take such opportunities rather than giving up or harking back to past arrangements and defective worldviews.

EXERCISE

1   Ask yourself in which way you are efficient in the world:
    What physical skills do you have (think of basic ones like walking and talking as well as more complex ones like typing, skating or swimming)? What gives you pleasure in terms of how you use your body in harmony with the physical universe?
2   Now describe to yourself how you create value with other people: what is your role in relation to others and how do you provide the world with added value?
3   What is cause for self-worth? How have you shown yourself to be a separate and worthy human being? How do you live in such a way that your life could be considered to be that of a person who deserves respect?
4   Finally ask yourself what the purpose of your life is. What is it you aim to accomplish by the end of your life: how will your life have made, even a small difference to the world?

Paradox and dilemma

The paradox of the spiritual world is that the realization there is no ultimate value system means that if we are to live a meaningful life we have to make our own.

The unsolvable dilemma is that even as we gain perspective on ourselves and life and come to accept the relativity of existence, we continue to desire ultimate meaning and purpose.

The basic question clients address in this dimension are: 'How should I live?'
And it is often evaded and denied by:

• Adopting a belief system that provides wholesale answers to all of our predicaments.
• Wishful thinking, for example, pretending that all people are good or that certain people are good and others are bad. This may be simple and easy but leads to confusion.
• Hopelessness and despair.
• Either/or thinking: attributing all that is good to one side of the universe and all that is bad to the other.

Denying the dilemmas of the spiritual world always leads to confusion which may be felt either as an acute crisis or like a consistent dull ache, a sense of dis-ease. It is as difficult to think about as it is crucial. It is our centre of gravity. Life may not have a god-given meaning and purpose, but it still works better when we are able to give it meaning and purpose.

The sort of questions that people ask themselves and their therapists at times of turmoil are:

- Why me?
- Am I being punished for something I did wrong?
- Am I a bad person if bad things keep happening to me?
- Is there any meaning or purpose in life if I feel I cannot control it and fate seems so fickle and unreliable?

These are all philosophical questions that require careful contemplation rather than quick answers.

ILLUSTRATION

WORKING WITH THE SPIRITUAL/ETHICAL DIMENSION

Amanda could not understand why she kept experiencing so many difficulties in her life. She had, she thought, lived an exemplary life, but had only been rewarded with some remarkable catastrophes. Her parents had divorced when she was just about to go to university, spoiling her pleasure at finding her independence from the battles her parents had fought when she was at home. She had always mediated in their conflicts, as being an only child she had given herself the purpose of keeping them together. She had tried to be fair to each of them, even though she thought them very childish in their behaviour. Her mother had made a fool of herself falling for a rich guy who was just having a bit of fun and who had left her mother promptly after dad had left her and she had become a liability. Her father, in an act of revenge had an affair with a young woman hardly older than Amanda, who he had ended up marrying, probably because he could not think of any other way to conclude the relationship. Ever since his remarriage he had been extremely unhappy and had come to Amanda for solace. Her mother would not speak to him and Amanda was really fed up with their 'stupid antics', as she called them. She took the view that having parents that were so irresponsible was a great misery, which had led to her own boyfriend leaving her, because he thought her far too closely involved with her father. She thought this was extremely childish behaviour on his part, since all she was doing was trying to mend her parents' marriage. She had come to consult a student counsellor at university because she wanted to understand why she had been cursed with such idiotic parents and boyfriend. After two sessions she decided to arrange for her parents to meet without them realizing this is what she was doing and she set them up with a double blind date which was in fact a date with each other. She was run over by a motorbike as she was waiting near the restaurant where her parents were to meet, where she tried to spy on them to see whether they were talking to each other. Her parents saw the ambulance take her into hospital but they did not realize it was their daughter who had just had an accident across the road from the restaurant. Amanda spent many weeks in hospital and only came back to counselling several months later, for she had had serious injuries, including a broken leg and a broken rib. She had been thinking about the miseries in her life and had wondered whether there was a god arranging all this. She was not so sure any more that she had always been exemplary and had begun to think that perhaps the opposite was true and that she was being punished for interfering in her parents' life. Her counsellor neither reassured her on this point, nor reassured her that she had in truth been exemplary and did not deserve her fate. Instead she helped her to think about the way in which all these events might or might not be connected and helped her elucidate how her own actions and interventions may have influenced the situation. It was crystal clear to Amanda that her hanging around across the road from the restaurant had directly led to the accident since she had constantly stepped into the road from which she could see inside of the restaurant where her parents were. She accepted that her hazardous conduct had caused the accident, even though the motorcyclist had been held responsible by the police and had in fact been over the limit. Upon reflection, she could see that there was a dual cause to the accident and that accidents often do occur when several things go wrong at the same time. She became worried about the motorcyclist's fate, for he had had his licence taken away and now she felt guilty for harming him. Her preoccupation with all these moral issues led to her taking an interest in ethics and reading up on it a bit. She began to question her interference with her parents' marriage and her judgements of their bad behaviour, but she also began to wonder whether the way life worked was actually very fortunate in that apparently one was constantly given new chances to come to terms with one's mistakes.

Commentary

Amanda benefited enormously from counselling during these difficult months and she used it to form a much clearer view of morality, purpose and meaning in life. She felt as if an opportunity had presented itself to her to understand what was wrong with the way she had been with her parents and because of that also with her boyfriend. She began experimenting with different ways of thinking and acting and found it gratifying that she seemed to acquire a lot of new friends who had similar interests.

KEY POINTS

- A value of existential therapy is that it is important that clients are able to discover for themselves how they wish to live – establishing their own value system. In order for existential therapists to facilitate this in their clients, they need to have done it for themselves and also to know what it is like to continually re-evaluate their value system in the light of circumstances and their place in life.

- Spirituality is not reserved for religion, but extends to any views and beliefs we hold about the world and an enquiry into the spiritual dimension is an enquiry into personal meaning consistent with the givens of existence.

- Such beliefs influence the way we conduct ourselves and the way we make sense of the world and gaining clarity about our values, beliefs and purpose is always valuable in making our lives come together.

- Values and beliefs are the basis of our role in the universe and are present in all our statements and actions, but they may not be easily put into words, indeed, there are some that may not be possible to put into words.

- The spiritual dimension is most likely to be addressed indirectly in therapy, by the client re-evaluating what is really important to them. This will either lead to a change in what they value or to a renewed commitment to a previous value. It is not likely to be addressed intellectually or by a discussion of philosophy. For meaning and purpose to be realized, a principle has to be lived and then evaluated.

- Where a person is in their life – how old they are – will lead them to value different aspects of life and to understand wisdom differently.

- A client may be experiencing difficulties in their life because of outdated or conflicting values.

- In therapy, the aim is always ultimately to help a person get clearer vision of what is going on, even, or perhaps especially, when it is not a pretty picture. But clearer vision is not the be all and end all, for sometimes it is better for a person to remain protected for a while. When a person is in a state of grief or is traumatized, the last thing they need is for us to open their eyes even wider. They need to be allowed a rest and we simply provide them with the safety in which they may find enough peace to become whole and strong again.

- We can never be certain about what may give meaning and purpose, but we can be certain that people who live without meaning and purpose do not flourish and that people who manage to create meaning even in difficult conditions thrive. This is directly relevant to therapy since it means making the search for meaning an aim for therapy rather than the search for symptom relief or the search for happiness.

- It is on the spiritual dimension that a person gains the greatest intensity of paradox, of being between life and death, of being alone and together, of being free and constrained.

7

THE PROCESS OF EXISTENTIAL THERAPY

When I let go of what I am, I become what I might be.
Lao Tzu

There are as many different issues as there are clients but what we consider in this chapter is that in spite of this, there are many similarities between clients with respect to the therapy process. We will consider what factors affect this and how the knowledge of this can help us to do therapy better. We will also see how all these matters affect therapists at least as much as clients.

EXISTENTIAL THERAPY AS STORYTELLING

On the simplest level, the therapist and client are just two people in a room telling a story to one another. Clients tell the story of what is important to them and how they came to be the person they are now and often their stories have gaps, either of time – some periods of their lives appear to have been forgotten, or of meaning – normally significant events like the death of a parent appear to have gone unnoticed. The therapist tells stories based on her understanding of the client's world and these are inevitably informed by her life experience and her existential interests. These have to be monitored and bracketed.

We all like to tell and to listen to stories. It is how we relate to each other. Some of the stories we tell are in order to entertain, some are in order to get insight but they are all in order to share and come to a joint understanding of life events. The therapist needs to understand that different clients and cultural groups have different narrative styles, different ways of telling stories and it is up to us as therapists to remember this and not to try to define the right way of telling a story.

Our task as therapists is not to shore up the current story or to find another story that fits. The task can be better understood by changing the noun 'story' into the verb 'to story', in a similar way that we changed 'self' to 'selve' earlier. What the therapist and client do is to re-story the client's experience so that new possibilities can be entertained and alternative meanings can be owned. It is about being able to make and to break narratives. It involves discovering that life is in flux, historical and dynamic, so that one story may be a good way of understanding events now, but not in a year's time. It involves trusting another person, the therapist, enough so that alternatives can be entertained without fear that the therapist will impose their own story on the client and constrain their emerging autonomy.

It is about the paradox of choosing and committing to a course of action in the full knowledge that one's knowledge can only be partial.

KEY POINTS

- Different people have different ways of telling stories.
- By attending, clarifying and verifying, the therapist facilitates the client to understand their life in different ways.
- There may be more than one way of understanding life events.
- We come to realize that we can endlessly transform our lives and with it the stories we tell about them.

MEETING, ASSESSMENT AND DIAGNOSIS

Therapy begins even before the two people meet for the first time. For the client, it begins when they start to ask themselves questions about their life. The moment they consider what they want and how they may get it, their therapy has started – even before they have found a therapist. For the therapist it begins when they ask themselves what they can expect to accomplish as a therapist. Every therapy benefits when the therapist questions themselves in this way.

Coming closer to the first session it evolves into the client thinking how they may be perceived and received by their therapist. Every client will wonder whether to risk saying the things they usually keep to themselves. Although they may be close to despair, they will also have some hope that coming to therapy will make a difference for the better. Above all, the client knows that they will not just be talking about difficult issues, they also know that they will be talking to another person who will be giving them their full and whole attention. This is not something we often obtain from another person and it can be both scary and attractive. The therapist for their part will also be wondering how the two of them will get on. With every new client an entirely new relationship is created and we can never take it for granted that it will work. Paradoxically, the more experience a therapist has, the less she may be able to remember what the first session is like for a client. It may be the first time a particular client has been to a therapist but for that therapist it may be the 200th time they see a client for the first time. Experienced therapists need to remember this. It takes a few moments of preparation to ready yourself for a new client. But the same can be said for seeing any client, since in a sense every client is a new client whether or not it is their first session.

EXERCISE

Try to remember (or imagine) the first time you went to a therapist:

- What did you think and feel before you arrived at the therapist's consulting room?
- And afterwards?
- What did you expect?
- What was your experience?
- Why did you go back?

Cohn (1997) says that assessment in existential psychotherapy is not possible because there is nothing to assess. He goes on to say that 'the client you meet is the client who meets you' (p. 33). What he means is that the quality of each session is so particular to time and place that any generalization will distract from the creation of a therapeutic relationship. Any assessment for therapy is inevitably saturated with the qualities of the assessor and most probably in ways they are unaware of. Existential therapists who work in settings where they receive formal assessments of their future clients frequently find a disparity between the description of the client in the assessment and their own perception of the same client. Nevertheless, even when there is no formal assessment, there is still some informal assessment. For as soon as two people meet, especially in a therapeutic relationship, they will try to get a measure of the other person and to gauge how the relationship may develop. This is mutual and will evolve over the weeks and months. In some ways this changing mutual evaluation and understanding are what focuses the relationship and what allows change to occur.

With respect to diagnosis, although existential therapists do not accept the medical principles of diagnosis, they will invariably work in settings that require or refer to diagnoses and they will often see clients who are familiar with diagnosis, even if these are only self-diagnoses. Existential therapists will rarely willingly comply with diagnostic activities, though in their training they will have had an opportunity to critically engage with existing categories of psychopathology, so that when they do they will be fully aware of the issues around diagnosis. The objective in existential therapy is to understand and actively engage with the way the client experiences issues and difficulties in their life, no matter how these have been diagnosed. The accuracy of any diagnosis given is always secondary to the meaning of the diagnosis for the client. What matters more than anything is how the person actually experiences the world.

KEY POINTS

- An assessment done by one person will be different from an assessment done by another.
- Assessment in existential therapy is mutual, both the therapist and client assess each other.
- Assessment is on-going and focuses on meaning and understanding rather than on diagnosis.
- Getting to grips with how our client experiences the world is what matters.

NOTE TAKING

It is compulsory in some work settings to make notes for the use of the work setting. It is good practice to summarize your experience of each session in writing. It is difficult to use supervision effectively without detailed notes and it is also not possible to write a case study without them. Our memories are not that good or reliable. You may at some point be required to testify about what happened in a session and keeping notes helps you to be realistic about the work you do. Notes should be made as soon as possible after the session to capture the feelings evoked by the session. Sensations and feelings will be forgotten first, then thoughts and finally actions. Notes can be about thoughts, feelings, questions, impressions, hunches, the client's purpose and problems, but may also particularly involve small excerpts of dialogue.

If you work with 50-minute sessions, that leaves you ten minutes to write your notes and reflect on your work. If ten minutes is not enough, you can fill your notes out later. Jotting down what you want to remember of a session makes it easier to move on to the next client. Having the notes reinforces the experience of the session and makes it more likely to be recalled in the next session. The act of writing notes is different from the act of reading notes. It is often enough to write them. Reading the notes of the previous session immediately before the next session can sometimes be useful if we need to recall a detail, but it can also prevent the therapist from being with the client in the present, concentrating too much on the previous week.

KEY POINTS

- Making notes is a part of being an effective and professional practitioner.
- They help you focus on the substance of each session, teaching you to summarize and clarify.

THE INFLUENCE OF THE FRAME AND THE CONTEXT OF THERAPY

There are three influences on the therapeutic relationship that affect it and give it its particular characteristics:

- *What the client brings.* This includes the client's history and their hopes and fears for the future. It includes their expectations of the therapy and of the therapist. The client's bias might also touch off specific reactions in the therapist.
- *What the therapist brings.* This includes the therapist's personal history and aspirations as well as their theoretical background. Their bias may also affect the client in particular ways.
- *The characteristics of the context of the therapy.* This includes:
  - the occupational setting – therapy in a doctor's surgery will take on different characteristics from that, for example, in an alcohol agency, even if the therapist and the client are the same;
  - the effect of payment;
  - the location, decoration and layout of the room – whether it is a designated room in a private house or a multi-purpose room in an institutional setting;
  - the time of day the sessions take place in – a session at 8am will be different from a session with the same person at the same place at 8pm. It is harder for some clients to come to therapy at the beginning of the day. Others prefer it. Similarly with therapists.

For these reasons as well it is difficult to think of assessment as being any more than simply an impression of what one person experienced in the relationship at one particular time and place. Caution about jumping to conclusions is therefore a very important aspect of our therapeutic frame and boundaries.

In the broadest sense, a frame or boundary is a line marking where one thing stops and another begins. The frame round a painting tells the viewer where the painting stops and the wall begins and is often distinctive. Whereas the boundary between material objects is often clear, the boundaries between people are much less obvious and often fluid. Nevertheless the therapy can only work if the therapist and client are clear about their roles. It is the therapist's task to remain a therapist and to be available for the client in their understanding of their life. Nevertheless, we know that people do not thrive when subject to inappropriate or insecure boundaries and each setting will bring a different set of boundaries which will make a difference to the qualities of the work.

EXERCISE

The effect of the setting on the therapy

Fill out the chart below and think about how the answers contribute to the nature of the work in each setting. Referral means how the client got to the agency. Payment means whether there is payment, how much, and who pays and who decides. Confidentiality refers to who is legally bound to know about what is said in sessions. Issue means what the client comes to the therapy to talk about. The settings in the left-hand column and the issues on the top of the chart are just examples. There are many more. Only the first row has been completed.

(Continued)

(Continued)

	Referral	Payment	Confidentiality	Issue	Contract length
General Practice	By the doctor in the practice	None	Within the primary care team	General, but usually not chronic anxiety	6 to 12 sessions
Alcohol agency					
Prison					
Bereavement agency					
Private Practice					

KEY POINTS

- The context of the therapy has at least as much influence on the therapy as either the therapist or the client.
- It is important to keep track of the frame and boundaries of the setting, if we want to have clarity about how we influence the client.

THE FIRST SESSION AND THE CONTRACT

As already said, the first session is characterized by a mutual checking out by the therapist and client of each other. This can be seen in terms of a number of tasks, that the therapist needs to do:

1 Establish rapport.
2 Get a measure of how the client thinks about themselves and their issues – what they already know and what they wish to know.
3 Ask the question 'Why now?' Issues may have been present in the client's life for a long time and we need to know what it is that has brought them to therapy now. The greater the awareness of this, the more likelihood there will be of a determination to work.
4 Find out the client's ability to be challenged about their assumptions.

5 Start to think existentially about the issues that are being brought. Are any of the four worlds over- or under-represented? What level of responsibility does the client feel they have for their lives?

6 Monitor their own reaction to the client and their story.

7 Come to some tentative conclusions about how the work will proceed, including number of sessions.

8 Decide whether referral is a better option.

9 Complete all the administrative tasks necessary for the smooth running of the therapy.

10 Find out how they feel about the session they have just had. It is useful to ask the client at the end of the first session the following, 'What's it been like to talk to me for the last 45 minutes?' If, for example, the client's issue is about relationships with older men and the therapist is an older man, this can be modified to 'What's it been like to talk to me, an older man, for the last 45 minutes?' The response to this can be illuminating. Consider the differences between the following responses which would not have been gained had the question not been asked.

- 'It's been good, I didn't think I'd be able to open up to someone like you, so soon.'
- 'OK, I've said pretty much everything I thought I would say.'
- 'What's that got to do with it? I've come here so you can help me sort out my problems.'
- 'Interesting. I chose you because you saw my friend, but it turned out to be very different to how I expected.'

EXERCISE

Sit in the chair your clients sit in and imagine sitting in that chair for the very first time being listened to by you.

- What is it like?
- What do you need?

In answer to questions about how the therapy will proceed, it is generally not useful to talk about theory or existential philosophy as this can be a distraction from the task in hand. Clients have a right to know what to expect and something like the following may be found useful.

'Although this is the first session and it is slightly different because of that, the other sessions will be similar in that you are here to talk and to think about your immediate issues, some of which you've talked about today and also what you want to do in life. I am here to listen and to help you to clarify and think with you about the things that matter. This may well involve things coming up that you had not thought of or would rather not think of and may also bring up difficult thoughts and feelings.

Being in therapy is a bit like doing a very big jigsaw puzzle. The pieces are yours, but although you do not have a clear idea of the picture that the puzzle makes, I believe that you know what it is or what you want it to be. You certainly know more about this than I do. What I know is how jigsaw puzzles sometimes fit together and where the pieces are likely to connect. So what we do here is a cooperative effort, where we look at the pieces and see how they may fit together, except the pieces are your thoughts and feelings about what you hope and fear and desire.'

Many existential therapists are in private practice and need to find a way to make a clear and explicit contract with their clients. Contracts will also often be used by voluntary and statutory agencies. It is good practice to provide the client with a clear information leaflet and to use a written contract which indicates what is expected of client and therapist and to ask the client to sign a consent form that states that they have read and accepted the conditions of the therapy.

The information given to the client should include:

- the qualifications of the therapist, their training, professional body and insurance;
- the location and timings of the therapy;
- the fee payable and the conditions of payment that are expected;
- the ways in which sessions will be contracted and may be cancelled;
- the rules around confidentiality, disclosure and referral that apply;
- some guidelines for how sessions may be of most benefit to the client.

The purpose of the contract is to make sure that all the boundaries of the work, time, cost, payment time, policy on absences, purpose, are in place and are known and agreed by both the therapist and client at the start of the work.

KEY POINTS

- The first session is different from all the rest.
- A written contract is a useful way of clarifying important administrative and ethical issues.

LENGTH OF THE CONTRACT

Because it is based on phenomenology, existential therapy can be adapted to fit the time available.

If there are 12 or fewer sessions available, homework, in the form of a reading, journal-writing or film watching project between sessions may be considered, simply to focus and make the best use of the time available. For example, *The Art of Loving* by Erich Fromm, or *Love and Will* by Rollo May are useful to start a client thinking about their relationships. Importantly though, such homework will always arise out of the work currently being done and will not be predetermined. While longer-term therapy will enable a full and wide-ranging existential analysis, in general, the shorter the contract, the greater will be the necessity to focus on just one or perhaps two related issues and because of this the therapy may resemble a coaching relationship. This may also happen if sessions are spaced out more than fortnightly.

Very often, and this would apply as much to short-term as to long-term work, clients find it valuable to write an account of their therapy and to make it a part of the therapy as well as being an intimate record of an important time in their life.

KEY POINTS

- The flexible nature of phenomenology means that it can be adapted to all varieties of contract.
- Clarity is of the essence.

FEES

Many therapists find the discussion of fees difficult. It is hard for therapists to put a monetary value on their care and attention without feeling they are demeaning it or exploiting the client. Nevertheless the money that changes hands, either directly or indirectly – since no therapy is actually free – has a powerful symbolic value. It clarifies that the relationship is a transaction between one person and another and reinforces the continuity of the work. Everything in our culture has a monetary value and this is how we express what something is worth. It is not an issue that can be ducked. Psychotherapy is a profession and this means the therapist needs to be able to earn a living. It is therefore crucial for the therapist to clarify for themselves what their position is on their monetary worth. They should carefully cost their own work in relation to their standard of living and the number of hours they are able and willing to work. If the therapist is unclear, it will reverberate through the work and the therapy will run the risk of being derailed because of the therapist's diffidence. If they charge too little to cover their overheads, they will feel resentful and become lazy and seek other gratifications from the client. If they find they are charging more than the client can afford, the client will be resentful and leave or the therapist may feel they have to give better value for money that will lead them into doing more and taking more responsibility for the client than is healthy. It is important that the client feels that the transaction, the relationship, between themselves and the therapist is fair and equitable. Correct payment enables this and prevents the client from feeling either resentful or indebted to the therapist.

Discussion of the meaning of money can rarely be done in the first session and may only come to light subsequently. Nevertheless the therapist has to be alert to the implications. Money is also important because existential autonomy – the ability to make and own one's decisions and actions – is correlated with economic independence – the ability to work and to earn one's own living and support oneself and contribute to the support of others. One of the authors (MA) found that clients who did not pay for counselling in general practice not only had greater absenteeism but also were more likely to give a present at the end of the work than clients in private practice, indicating both that counselling was given a lesser value and also that the clients felt more indebted to the counsellor.

KEY POINTS

- Many people, including therapists, find handling money difficult.
- It is important for many reasons to establish firm agreements on payment.

THE BEGINNING AND END OF SESSIONS

If the client comes at the same time each week we must remember that 167 hours will have passed since the last session. This means that a great deal may have happened between sessions and we must resist the temptation to assume the client is preoccupied with the same issue as the week before. We must also resist the temptation to begin the session by asking about something just because we are interested in it. Therefore the client should be encouraged to begin with whatever they are preoccupied at that moment. In this way the client's autonomy is reinforced. Over the course of time, as clients get used to taking charge of their sessions they will get better at thinking between sessions as well, and the sessions will join up. Some clients do this very quickly, others less so and therapists can actively encourage this process by making links between themes pursued in different sessions. This is also the purpose of homework, to help the sessions join up and become more productive. Ideally, phenomenologically, we would allow the sessions to unfold at their own speed but often the constraints of the setting and contract mean that we can make modifications to technique and suggest, but not dictate, a starting point.

The position on the end of sessions is similar. Life is continuous and therapy only takes up a small but significant part of life. The temptation for the therapist to use the last few minutes of the session to summarize in order to reduce ambiguity and treat the therapy as something distinct from the rest of life should be resisted. It is likely to reduce the client's own analytic capacity. It may well be that what is being considered is not ready to be summarized anyway, in which case to do so would be inappropriate.

Many existential therapists ensure that the client has sight of the clock in the session and it then becomes the existential therapist's responsibility simply to point out that the time is up.

ILLUSTRATION

THE BEGINNING OF A SESSION

Session 3

Client: I don't know what to talk about today. What were we talking about last week?

Therapist: What do you remember?

Client: I don't know, what was it? Do you remember?

Therapist: If I said what I remembered, it may not be what was significant for you, bearing in mind that you were probably thinking and feeling many things that did not get put into words.

> *Client.* Hmm.
>
> *Therapist.* What's it like to come here, talk about important matters and then forget them? It's important for you to remember?
>
> *Client.* Well, yes. I feel disjointed ... yes, that's what I was talking about ... feeling disjointed.
>
> **Commentary**
>
> By staying with the client's current experience and resisting the request to remember the last session, which may well have not been what the client remembered, the client was able to recall a significant issue, which was the reason she had forgotten.

Door-handle comments

On some occasions the client says something between the formal end of the session, between when the therapist says 'We have to stop for today' and when they leave the room. This may be something like 'Oh, I forgot, I can't come for the next 2 weeks' or 'Your job looks easy, how do you get to be a therapist?' or 'I don't know how you put up with seeing people like me all the time, it would drive me around the bend.'

We can call these sorts of comments 'door-handle comments' because they are usually said with one hand on the door handle. They are often highly significant because they are invariably about both how the client sees their relationship with the therapist and also issues that were not discussed in the session, possibly because the therapist was following her own agenda. They are always difficult and the response calls for extreme sensitivity, but the therapist needs to take note of them and try to find a way to weave them into the next session. They are only outside the session because the client was not able to find a way to put them in the session.

KEY POINTS

- The client must be encouraged to set the agenda.
- What is said at the very beginning of the session before the formal start of the session, and at the end after the formal end of the session, is usually highly significant.
- Breaks and holidays should be mentioned in good time and also at the start of the session.

WORKING THROUGH, RELUCTANCE AND RESISTANCE

What we mean existentially by working through is the active process of addressing the obstacles one puts in one's own way, and as Nietzsche said, accepting reality for what it is. Overcoming resistance hinges on the ability to accommodate the anxieties elicited by unexpected interpretations and involves working through the unavoidable fear of coming to terms with who we are, what others make of us and the impact of chance. When we dare to face what we are and what life brings, everything comes clear and we can actually start to live without holding back the whole time.

This does not mean that once we accept our vulnerability, our resistance immediately diminishes. In therapy, working through entails persevering with the work of therapy as best one can, despite inevitable obstacles. In working through, disowned experience becomes owned and changes one's way of seeing the world.

The difference between reluctance and resistance is that while the reluctant client is likely to know what they are avoiding, and deliberately not talk about it, the resistant client is likely to be unaware of the significance of their avoidance and will therefore dismiss the possibility without considering it first. Existentially it is an issue of how open the client is to alternatives. We need to be careful that we do not label as resistance every example of when the client does not agree with something we say. It is quite possible that we are wrong.

ILLUSTRATION

RELUCTANCE AND RESISTANCE

Uncharacteristically, a client did not attend their previous session and also did not let their therapist know.

Client: I'm sorry I didn't come last week, I was held up at work.
Therapist: You seem to have a lot of hold-ups at work at the moment.
Client: Yes I do.
Therapist: What was it like not being able to come?
Client: What do you mean?
Therapist: I wondered if you didn't come to the last session not so much because you were busy, although I'm sure you were, but because you were angry with what I said the last time we met.

If the therapist's assumption was wrong, the client would say:

Client: Oh that, yes, I was hurt at first, but then I thought about it and realized you had a point but I was busy at work – I'm sorry I didn't let you know.

The reluctant client would say:

Client: Ah, yes, I wondered if you knew … I was really … it was when you said … and I found it difficult to know what to do when I feel like that. I thought I'd ignore it and hope it would go away.
Therapist: And has it?

> *Client:* I hoped it had … oh dear, obviously not. I've actually been thinking about it all the time since. I wondered if I'd talk about it. OK here goes … I was really upset and angry when you said …

But the resistant client would say:

> *Client:* No, I don't think so, I don't remember what we were talking about now, I was just very busy, it's that new project I told you about, it's been crazy at work, that's really all it was.

KEY POINT

- Existentially, working through is about staying with our anxiety until in can be tolerated and understood as a part of living.

ENDINGS AND TERMINATION

Compared with the amount written on the start and the maintenance of therapeutic relationships, the amount written on endings is almost insignificant and it is hard not to put this down to a universal avoidance of the issue of death and endings.

In some ways, brief existential work reflects the human condition because awareness of death is present in therapy by the ending of the contract. The end is in sight as soon as we have started and this itself can be effective in helping people to wake up and take charge of their lives and on occasions it may be enough. It can also focus the mind of the therapist.

It obviously means that we need to be mindful from the start of how we are going to end the relationship.

Many clients come to therapy with issues about unsatisfactory endings or losses and it is important that the client does not experience the end of the therapy as something else that ended unsatisfactorily.

It is the therapist's responsibility to know how to provide a constructive new model that tailors the work so that they get to the end of the work at the end of the time. As with loss and bereavement, the termination of therapy is not just a cessation of activity, it is a process to be worked through. Both the task − what they came to do or understand, and the relationship issues − the fact that they shared these important issues with the therapist as another person, need to be addressed.

Whatever the contract, it is recommended that no less, and in many cases more, than one-sixth of the total time together is spent considering the ending. With a fixed term contract, the decision of when to stop is taken away but what remains is to work out how to evaluate and end it. Therefore, clients who have a particular sensitivity to loss and endings will need more time and care in working through the implications of the ending. In these cases the whole time may be spent considering the ending.

Placing an emphasis on the number of sessions left and monitoring its meaning will reduce the likelihood of premature termination.

Given that endings are universally difficult, with an open-ended contract the issue for both the therapist and client is to arrive at an ending which is at the right time for both of them. This can only be known by the two people on the basis of their work together, but in assessing the end it is useful to bear in mind the risks and signs of poorly managed endings, which are characterized by:

- the client leaving suddenly;
- leaving when either the outcome of the task and/or the relationship has not been evaluated;
- leaving with a denial of feelings of loss;
- ending after a specific goal has only been partially met;
- leaving before the work has had a chance to establish itself.

The therapist has to be able to face endings themselves with openness and to know when they either prolong or shorten the ending for their own reasons. Supervision is very important in throwing light on these blind spots.

As therapy is about relationship as well as task, the client will probably wish to know that the therapist will remember them in future and would be happy to see them again if they were to return. Giving the client this sense of being valued is less likely to come about simply by saying so. It is more likely to be reinforced by the quality of the therapist's attention over the whole time and especially at the end. Often the way the client will remember the therapy will be related to the nature of this ending, for it is in the end that they are sent on their way to take charge of whatever problems their life brings and it creates the final sense of what has been achieved. The better the ending, the more the work will be remembered as valuable and the gains sustainable.

It is not the job of the existential therapist to advise the client to stay or to go, but to ensure that the reasons for staying or for going are sufficiently examined. Whether it is an appropriate decision or not cannot be known unless the issue is discussed.

To this end, if a client is reluctant to discuss a sudden departure, the likelihood is that the ending will not be well managed, but if they will discuss it, the likelihood is that it will be well managed.

Nevertheless, it is important to remember that since life is constantly unfolding there can be no point at which any therapy can be said to have finished – it can only ever be enough for the time being.

In the final analysis, only clients themselves can know what is right or wrong for them at any one time, though therapists would fail in their duty of care if they did not challenge or carefully examine sudden decisions to relinquish the work.

EXERCISE

- Think of something that ended 'well'.
- Think of something that ended 'badly'.
- What did you think, feel and do, before, during and after each of these examples?

- How did you prepare for them (if you did)?
- Was your involvement active or passive?
- What did you learn about the way you manage endings?

KEY POINTS

- The end of the therapy begins at the beginning of the therapy and is worked on throughout therapy.
- Many people including therapists find endings difficult, so that they avoid facing them squarely.
- The nature of the ending of therapy can be the benchmark by which the client remembers the therapy.
- It is important to think through the therapeutic relationship and its ending and model good endings for the client.

THERAPY AS A LEARNING PROCESS

Being a client in psychotherapy is about learning how to live more effectively and discovering strengths as well as weaknesses. It is about finding out what obstacles one puts in the way of getting what one claims to want and it is an emotional task, an existential task, more than it is a technical or intellectual task.

Although we usually move in the direction of greater competence, events outside of our control occur that make us feel considerably less competent that we thought we were. Resilience in the face of life's slings and arrows is constantly tested and we continue learning throughout our professional career. It also applies equally to therapist and client.

In therapy the client not only has to learn the skills of living more resourcefully but they also have to learn the skill of using therapy. It is easy for therapists to forget this.

The process of acquiring skills is marked by a characteristic sequence of thoughts, feelings and actions that can evolve backwards and forwards through what can be thought of as four qualitatively different phases. However, each contains and is as important as the other and the significance of all have to be acknowledged in order that learning be consolidated and owned.

First phase

The starting point for many clients is when they know that things are not working for them, but generally feel unable to make any changes.

This phase can be summarized as: 'There are a lot of things I don't know but I don't know what they are.'

The feelings at this time can be:
- excitement – at finally deciding to do something about it;
- anxiety, fear and apprehension – at what they may discover;
- curiosity – at finding out something new;

- but they may also be in a state of despair or discouragement about life in general and their own life in particular;
- in this case they may feel little hope for the future. This is where they are in the first session and often for some considerable time.

Our task during this time is mainly to listen and clarify. By our clarifying, the assumptions that led to the client seeking therapy begin to come to light and we make explicit what is hidden. We begin to get an idea of how they inhabit and organize their physical, social, personal and spiritual dimensions. We get a sense of how they see themselves in the world, how they see their relationships, how they see themselves as active agents and what their values are.

Second phase

Gradually, as they talk, and we listen, and they listen to themselves, and they experience themselves being listened to by us, and they wonder about the significance of what they are saying, they get an enhanced awareness of their position in life.

This phase can be summarized as: 'I now know a great deal more about what I don't know.'

This can be a very difficult stage of therapy and many clients can be tempted to leave at this point. The sort of things clients say are:

- I came here to feel better but I'm feeling worse.
- You are really trying to help me, but I realize I just cannot do it, it is too difficult and I will just keep getting it wrong.

Or they may say:

- This is extraordinary, I always knew there was stuff going on I had no idea of, and at long last I'm beginning to get a handle on it.

The sort of feelings that come up here are:

- anxiety – at facing the void of not knowing and of having to take responsibility for their own way of being, but also at finding out things they did not want to find out;
- frustration – at not feeling able to do anything about it;
- cynicism – at why should things be any better than this;
- guilt and blame – at how they have led their lives;
- 'sour grapes' – they may say they are not very interested anyway, they can get along quite well without it.

They may also say that therapy is 'boring'. This use of 'boring' means anything but uninteresting and dull. It means there is too much going on and that it is new and doesn't yet make sense. It means they feel overwhelmed by the complexity of their feelings, that then turn to a kind of fog. Facing our ignorance can be extremely unsettling as the foundations of what we thought was so are questioned. Calling therapy boring is a way at keeping our anxiety at bay in the face of emergent change.

Our task here is to try to understand this anxiety, both intellectually and emotionally. This is a necessary step as the client begins to tolerate their anguish, to come face to face with the human condition and begins to understand it differently. At this point we will be making descriptive interpretations, which means that we verify and search for an accurate description of the client's experience that captures it without distorting it but that nevertheless brings it to light in a new way. Quite often it will mean bringing ambiguity to the fore and pointing out the paradoxes in the client's life, or how they repeat past patterns.

This too can be difficult for the therapist and they need to use their therapy and supervision to get some perspective and to learn to tolerate the anxiety which is an inevitable part of learning. The clients are facing the facts of life, and we need to bear with them as they pluck up the courage to begin the long journey of finding out what might need to change.

ILLUSTRATION

WANTING TO GIVE UP JUST WHEN IT GETS DIFFICULT

Session 12

Mick had come to therapy because of panic attacks. He had been to three therapists before but left them all after a few sessions. He said rather vaguely that he left because they had not helped him.

Mick: I don't know about this therapy ... it's not working. I keep on having the anxieties and I haven't learnt anything to stop them. All we do is talk ... I'd like to make this the last session.

Therapist: What's it like to be wanting to leave now?

Mick: OK.

Therapist: Just OK?

Mick: Erm, frustrating, disappointing.

Therapist: Because?

Mick: I won't have done anything about it ... it just seems too difficult ... I don't think I can be bothered.

Therapist: Bothered with?

Mick: All the going into it ... and thinking about everything again.

Therapist: Yes, I was wondering about that. That far from it being pointless to go on, perhaps there is rather too much point, so much so that it becomes distressing and that you are afraid to tackle it.

Mick: That's what one of my last therapists said too. Maybe there is something in it.

(Continued)

(Continued)

Commentary

The therapist decided to focus on the dilemma that Mick felt between wanting to stay and wanting to go in order that he might engage with it and discover for himself that he needed to do so and carry on. It would have been a mistake for the therapist to take at face value Mick's statement that he wanted to leave. It would also have been a mistake to persuade Mick to stay. Mick's autonomy had to be respected even though it may have been difficult for him to express it in a constructive way rather than in a self-destructive way.

Third phase

Gradually the client gets used to the new experience of thinking and feeling differently and the feelings at this time are likely to be:

- excitement — at something new having happened;
- optimism and hope that life might actually change for the better;
- and unease — because it is so unfamiliar and delicate and because changes for the better have never lasted before.

This phase can be summarized as: 'I know it's what I wanted and I can't really believe it and fear I will lose it again.'

Changes are still very new and cannot yet be owned. Clients may swing from hope to despair and may come back each week wielding proof of their incompetence, only to be quickly reminded of how they have actually handled their life far more effectively and creatively and so far more with awareness and courage than they ever did before.

ILLUSTRATION

GETTING USED TO DOING THINGS DIFFERENTLY

Session 18

Jane came to therapy because whenever she met a man she was interested in and she could tell was interested in her, she found herself unable to talk to him and usually 'made a fool' of herself, got embarrassed, often drank too much and this led to the end of the relationship before it had begun.

Jane: It was really weird because I was talking with David, who I've talked about, at lunch yesterday and I remembered everything we'd been talking about. I was being a different sort of me. I didn't

> say very much to him, but at least I didn't say anything stupid, and he was asking me things.
>
> *Therapist:* Like?
>
> *Jane:* Oh, where I was born, what I liked doing on holidays and at weekends, I thought he was going to ask me out.
>
> *Therapist:* What was it like?
>
> *Jane:* Good, scary, it was good, but a bit odd, it felt like he was interested in me, but I kept thinking it won't last, that it was only because he hadn't got anyone else to talk to, you know all the stuff we've been talking about that I do.
>
> *Therapist:* How did it feel that you were able to do something different?
>
> *Jane:* Yes, I suppose I did, didn't I? I did it. Like I had a new toy, and it was mine, and I deserved to have it, I didn't used to believe that. This is scary though. I'll probably mess it up tomorrow.
>
> *Therapist:* Who would?
>
> *Jane:* OK, OK, OK, the old me would do that, the one that's so stuck in the past and sabotages, doesn't believe in herself. I don't have to, do I?

Commentary

Jane was discovering how it felt to be doing things differently. This was in equal measures empowering and unsettling. Whereas she used to identify with her self-destructive potential, she was beginning to see that this was not actually what she wanted, it was just what she had previously become used to and was now in the process of disowning in favour of a way of being with her anxieties that acknowledged them rather than avoided them.

Our task at this point is to try to consolidate the changes made so they can be integrated into the person's idea of themselves. This often means pointing out how the client has actually done things differently, more competently, more courageously and more fairly to themselves and others. We need to be affirmative and sustaining of progress at this point.

Fourth phase

As the client gets used to doing things differently a more resilient excitement can appear which can be summarized as: 'I know how to do it now and I don't have to think about it.'

There is something particularly powerful about this but it also dangerous. Powerful because of the excitement of the feeling that the person can do something where before they were unable, but dangerous because the complacency can lead to arrogance, to hubris. This is a manic kind of power where the givens of existence are disregarded. This always leads to a fall.

ILLUSTRATION

CHALLENGING COMPLACENCY

Session 24

Anthony had been unemployed for some months after having been asked to leave previous jobs because of his unreliability. He had just been offered a job at a recent interview.

Anthony: Well, I love the job, so everything's going to be great now.

Therapist: I'm glad you got the job. How will you approach it, after what we know about how you sabotage things?

Anthony: Oh, it'll be fine, I just know it.

Therapist: How do you know it?

Anthony: What, are you saying I'll mess it up? I thought you believed in me. That's really disappointing.

Therapist: I'm not saying you will or that you will not, for I don't know. I certainly hope you won't. I'm just remembering that this is the sort of situation that has been difficult for you in the past and that it's important that you be aware of the traps you set yourself.

Anthony: Hmmm. I suppose you're right

Commentary

Anthony had come to the conclusion that as he now knew what he had been doing wrong before that it would not happen again. This is not necessarily so because we need to test ourselves in as similar a situation to the original one as possible before we can have any certainty of success. In many ways we can never take success for granted and have to remain attentive to all we do and think.

Our task here is to encourage the emerging competence and confidence while guarding against over-confidence, and sometimes the therapist can be seen as a bit of a kill-joy at this point.

The equivalent danger for the therapist is to begin to feel as if they know how to be a therapist and become complacent. This is the moment they will make a mistake and not realize that it is a mistake and see the consequences of it as the client's responsibility.

EXERCISE

This process is also a model of how therapists learn to be therapists. Remember back to when you started learning how to be a therapist or when you first went to your personal therapy:

- What was it like?
- How did it feel?
- What did you discover about how you learnt?
- What were the obstacles on the way?
- Did you want to give up?
- What made you carry on?

The final phase of therapy has already been discussed. It is a time when we summarize and transcend all the troubles and worries that have been worked through. Now the client thinks: 'I am as ready to live life as I will ever be, for I can deal with whatever may come.'

KEY POINTS

- Both therapist and client go through the same process when learning about life and about therapy.
- The key to understanding the way we learn is how we feel towards the process.
- Every new client is a challenge to our ideas of our competence.
- Learning skills is not a one-way process.
- We need different skills at different times.

8

PUTTING IT ALL TOGETHER: SUMMING UP

Become who you are.

Friedrich Nietzsche

SUMMARIZING THE PHILOSOPHICAL BASIS OF EXISTENTIAL PRACTICE

Although people wishing to work existentially do not necessarily need to know the literature in great detail, they do need some discipline and method in their philosophical thinking about the world. While there is much fertile debate among existential therapists about the detail of how the different philosophies can be applied to therapy, there is agreement on these basic existential principles.

In existential therapy:
- Personal problems can only be understood against the wider background of human living, and not purely as personal or intra-psychic issues.
- The search for well-being should be seen in relation to an understanding of the human condition, of life's contradictions, tensions and dilemmas.
- Meaning is sought in the client's particular predicaments, both in terms of their universal significance and their very individual and personal implications.
- There is a search for a model of living that can improve a person's life, without prescriptive endorsement of any particular model.
- There is an openness to understanding individual experience within a person's cultural, political and social context.

- There is a conviction that life's paradoxes and dilemmas must be faced dialectically and not avoided in order for a person to thrive.
- We engage in a form of applied philosophy whose medium is dialogue and which requires commitment and full engagement for success. It needs to comply with the rigorous standards of philosophical research. It involves testing out and verifying hypotheses about human living and revising these in the light of new findings.
- Any conclusions arrived at can only be provisional.
- Our practice is based upon the principles of phenomenology and consists of careful and exhaustive description of the experience leading to an understanding and verification of their implications and consequences.
- There is a belief that not only is it possible to make sense of life, but also that it is good to try to make sense of life.
- The philosophical responsibility of enabling clients to find direction and autonomy needs to be balanced with a clear sense of the necessary aspects of human living. Freedom without a sense of obligation, duty, or responsibility does not exist.
- To live with courage and confidence is to trust that we can always find a way to resolve our puzzles and overcome obstacles and difficulties no matter what comes on our path.
- A successful outcome is not to make people happy or to enable them to live such that problems no longer exist but to have the courage to experience all the challenges and difficulties that a life in flux inevitably produces.

SUMMARIZING THE PRINCIPLES OF EXISTENTIAL PRACTICE

We have seen how existential practitioners think about their work and how an existential attitude may be fostered and we have also demonstrated how wide-ranging and adaptable the existential approach is.

Many of the suggestions here are ways of thinking about your clients, and some will be more present than others. It is out of these that we make phenomenologically consistent interventions. They are also useful to bear in mind when bringing your work for existential supervision.

Collaboration, freedom and dialogue

Existential work is collaborative and relies on the alliance you create, not just with your client, but with your client in relation to life itself. Questions are asked with the client rather than of them and are designed to help them focus on the issue so that it stands out against the horizon of their world. Initially you are likely to ask few questions. Only when you know the question is one that will help the client explore their experience from a different angle, do you pose it, briefly and clearly, on their behalf. These prompts will often be something like: 'how do you mean?', 'can you give me an example?', 'what was that like?', 'what made you think this?', 'how did this happen?', 'for what purpose?', 'because …?', 'how?', 'in what context?', 'when exactly?'

With respect to freedom, we encourage clients to freely explore issues in terms of personal experience and not to give up as soon as a dilemma or a conflict is revealed.

The explicit, the implicit and self-deception

By clarifying the explicit, the implicit will be revealed. This is done by keeping interventions simple, short and few and by using the client's own words. As time goes on, the client's attention can be drawn to the dimensions of their experience that have become hidden and only implied. When there is a large and denied difference between the explicit and the implicit, they will be deceiving themselves about their part in their lives and hanging on to counterproductive beliefs or illusions.

Only make statements about self-deception when this arises as a clear issue in what is said or not said and always link it to purpose in order that your client's vision can be broadened to encompass a wider horizon. It is not about telling them they should look at things differently but it is a process of unfolding that can only be done with an attitude of openness and affirmation.

Themes and issues

In the early sessions you will be looking for the themes that stand out in the client's experience of the world. While clarifying, ask yourself:

- What is the theme?
- What is the client after or evading?
- How are they trying to be alive and fulfilled?

This systematic exploration will allow the client's worldview to gradually become clearer to both therapist and client and this will continue throughout therapy.

Values and beliefs

These relate to the spiritual dimension of existence and will be more implicit rather than explicit. In therapy we always start from the client's experience and uncover how their implicit beliefs and values determine the way in which they live their lives. The aim is for the client to be able to re-assess and own their values.

The four worlds

As you become more familiar with the client's themes and values, the four worlds framework can be used to understand their worldview. Each statement, attitude and experience can be seen in terms of these four dimensions and ask yourself – though not necessarily your client:

- What is implied about the physical and the natural world?
- What is happening in the client's social and public world?
- What kind of private and personal world does she inhabit?
- What are her values and beliefs in the ideal or spiritual world?

You may also wonder which are present, absent or problematic. In this process we become more aware of the tensions and paradoxes only implicit in our client's experience.

Projects, fears and tensions

You can ask yourself, in each dimension:

- What are their main concerns?
- What is their original project?
- What moods or emotions are referred to or are absent?

In this way, a fuller picture of the client's preoccupations emerges and we get a sense of what moves them, what stops them, what inspires them and what strengths they can build on and what fears might undermine them.

Complexity and subtlety

When you are at ease with the emerging but provisional picture of your client's worldview and grasp something of their existential dilemmas, you can begin to investigate their experience in more detail, probing for the complexities and subtleties.

Pace interventions faster when you aim for more focus, slower when you aim for a broader expression of experience. But always make sure you remain connected to what really matters to your client rather than to what you think they ought to feel or think. Remember you bracket your assumptions in order to maintain perspective and see the client's worldview in context.

Meaning

Meanings are implied and embedded in the client's words and it is for you to bring them out so they can be aware of them. Ask yourself constantly what the meaning of statements is: don't assume you know. Even when you do think you know, ask for confirmation. Such verification is an essential part of phenomenological work. Be disciplined in this process of checking back and refine your awareness of when you do not do it.

The client will usually be pleased to explore their understanding of the world as long as your interventions are made in the spirit of genuine collaboration and generosity.

It is part of the wider process of them gaining awareness of their own meanings and it helps them to re-examine these meanings occasionally rather than to take them for granted.

Paradox and conflict

Life is made of paradox and conflict – we get our energy from the tension between life and death. It cannot be evaded or denied, only met and worked with. Be sensitive to the client's understanding of paradox. It may be useful to point out that something good may have to be sacrificed for something better to emerge. That something new may lead to different dangers. And then polarities formerly seen as conflicts can be reframed in terms of dilemmas which need to be experienced before a resolution can be arrived at.

Truth, evaluation and verification

All existential work should be constantly checked and verified. Factual truth about what occurred in a client's life can rarely be checked but the truths about what happens between client and therapist can be and is an important way to check the process. The therapist and client will always understand the work differently. And this will be addressed in existential supervision. Another way the work can be verified is by the evidence of the client's new ways of being. Only if they find that their lives are more courageous, realistic and full, will we know that progress has been achieved.

An existential structural analysis

As a result of the above, you can gradually start to think about the basic structures of the client's existence:

- **Preconceptions and assumptions:** each assumption a client holds needs to be formulated and faced before it can be understood.
- **Beliefs and values:** the person's worldview is underpinned by beliefs, and these are related to what they value and hold dear. Be respectful of these various aspects of a person's views, while helping them to clarify them and make sense of them. Sometimes you need to challenge contradictions.

- **Choice points and decisions:** assumptions and values come clearly into play at times when decisions and choices have to be made. It is often when important decisions have to be made that the client's worldview becomes obvious and their strength is tested. It is then that clarity about the sort of choice they want to make is most needed.
- **Expectations and fears:** the individual viewpoint is most obscured by fears about the future, when the person is no longer sure about the outcome of their choices. Help them elucidate their expectations and determine what line of action is most suited to their new understanding of what truly matters in their life.
- **Projects and ideals:** the only way in which assumptions, beliefs, decisions and expectations can be realigned is when a person can commit herself to a new ideal that makes sense to her both intellectually and emotionally. Such an ideal will generate various projects in their life: an overall project that is about what they want to do before they die, but also a number of smaller projects, that are achievable in the short and medium term. All of these need to be in harmony with the person's sense of what is right and true.

DEVELOPING A PERSONAL STYLE

We have seen in these pages the existential approach is not only distinguished by its philosophical clarity but also by its directness. While some specific interventions are suggested in this book, the task for the aspiring existential practitioner is to develop their own style, but one which is based firmly on the principles described here. In existential therapy little is prescribed but this is not the same as saying that anything goes. Life is the teacher as well as the judge, and existential interventions always come out of an understanding of the human interaction between this particular client and this particular therapist at this particular time and place. What can be learnt in therapy, as in life, will always surprise us and it can never be fully summarized in books or in prescriptive teachings. Human beings have to keep searching to understand the realities of the human condition and of existence, rather than take it on authority from someone else without thinking.

We are all responsible for our own point of view and our own learning but we also have to acknowledge the autonomy of others. The difference between the person we are and the job we do as therapists is only in the constraints of the setting and the ethical boundaries. We are the sort of therapist we are because of the sort of person we are.

Like life, this takes a lifetime to get right.

GLOSSARY

Anxiety   is more than stress, depression or agitation. It is more like an apprehension: a basic background unease, which nevertheless can come to the fore and sometimes disables us in times of crisis. It involves a vague and discomforting awareness of the unsolvable dilemmas of existence and usually includes a non-specific sense of danger, a sense that we may die, that we are separate from other people, that we are responsible for our own lives, and that we may fail to live up to our own moral code. This specific form of anxiety is often termed existential anxiety and it is assumed that we cannot live without this form of essential discomfort, since it points us towards our fundamental freedom and responsibility, without which we would not have consciousness nor be human. In final analysis anxiety is our life energy.

Assumptions   Human beings are meaning-making creatures and cannot help but construct meanings in terms of the values, beliefs and meanings they already have. These meanings are simply assumptions that we have made in order to understand the world. Such assumptions help us make sense of things. By working phenomenologi-cally we can become more aware of the assumptions we habitually use to understand the world and we can sharpen our own capacity to question them, reflect on them and alter them as new information becomes available.

Authenticity/Inauthenticity   do not refer to what is real or genuine but instead to our ability to own and to be the author of our lives in full awareness that it will end and that it is up to us to make something of it. There is no such thing as an authentic act. Authenticity only arises when our attitude towards existence is one of facing truth and when we allow this stance of truth seeking to inform our actions. As such it is rarely sustainable and we inevitably come to deny our existential responsibility and so revert back to inauthenticity, which is our more usual mode of being. When this in turn becomes intolerable, we may once again respond to the call of conscience and own up to our responsibility. Authenticity and inauthenticity are two sides of the same coin and are inseparable.

Autonomy   refers to the basic desire and ability of human beings to make their own decisions about their lives and to be independent in their conduct and their thinking. Such self-motivated behaviour is never an excuse for ignoring other people's needs and views.

Bad faith (*mauvaise foi*)   is a term used by Sartre to refer to the way in which we actively evade and deny our freedom and our nothingness. To be in bad faith is to pretend to ourselves that we are either completely helpless and condemned to our fate or completely free and able to be just anything we choose.

Change is not something the existential therapist works to bring about. Since our basic nature is one of permanent change, what we work to bring about is an understanding of how clients habitually resist, evade and deny change in their lives so as to help them become aware of how they are avoiding making their own decisions and choices.

Choice and responsibility. An existential choice is about commitment to a course of action and is not always simply about selection between alternatives. On many occasions there is only one alternative on offer. It is about grasping life rather than evading and denying life. Responsibility is a central theme of existential thinking. It refers to an acknowledgement of personal accountability for one's choices and actions. This goes for those actions actively taken as well as for those which are attributed to our context or to contingency. It is important to note that abstaining from choosing is also a choice. The only choice we do not have is not to choose.

Crisis. A crisis is an opportunity and a moment when we realize not just the necessity of action but when we become aware of the fragility of existence. We also become aware that our future depends on what decision we make now. In a crisis we are called to account for ourselves and it is when we show our mettle. It is a time when we realize that we can never guarantee with any certainty what will happen. Every moment potentially has this quality but we habitually deny it, thinking that we are passive recipients of our lives rather than active creators.

Death marks the end of our physical life and is the boundary which informs all our decisions of how to live. Our life as a totality only becomes complete and therefore fully meaningful on death. Living with awareness of the temporal nature of our lives makes us aware of the urgency of living life to the full and makes it easier to appreciate what is truly of value.

Description/Explanation. A crucial distinction in existential practice. Description is central to phenomenology which asks us to bracket off our assumptions about the nature of something in favour of an experience-near description of what affects us. Asking clients to describe will enable them to get closer to the truth of their experience and hence uncover its meaning. Explanation will, on the other hand, promote a distancing and a more superficial understanding that will inevitably be in terms of someone else's understanding. Description reduces the influence of suggestion in therapy whereas explanation increases it.

Determinism. Human beings are undoubtedly moved and affected by numerous complex forces, in terms of our genes, our education and our character, but we are not entirely determined or caused by them. Human consciousness provides us with the capacity to take a particular attitude towards these givens and go beyond them in making sense of the world and also by affecting the way in which it will change in future. We make something of what has been made of us. We transform our world.

Dialectic is the way dilemmas are solved, by bringing together two apparent opposites to make something entirely new. It is not about compromise. Resolutions arrived at dialectically are never fixed but permanently changing. Each new formulation contains some of the former opposition while proposing a new idea. In dialectical living we are prepared to continuously evolve and develop while learning from the past.

Dialogue is the essence of therapy, human interaction and the source of human meaning. Buber says it is fleeting, challenging, difficult to achieve and sustain and can often become two simultaneous monologues. Heidegger refers to the absence of dialogue as 'idle talk'. To be in dialogue is to be interactively involved in our intersubjectivity and fully address each other and therefore come into our own and work our way through whatever it is we are speaking about and engaging with.

Dilemma. All the important questions in life involve a dilemma which cannot be solved with a simple yes or no, right or wrong. For their meaning to be revealed, the tension within the dilemma needs to be engaged with resiliently. The existential therapist's job is to promote this greater engagement with the tensions of the dilemma. This often involves making a person aware of the paradoxes of existence.

Embodiment is the term given to the principle that the body is not something I have, it is something I am. Perception, as Merleau-Ponty says, is only possible with and through the body that is permanently attuned to the world it is a part of. To be fully aware of something and experience and live it deeply and concretely rather than to have opinions or theories about it is to become fully embodied. This is engaged living.

Empathy in the sense of being able to 'stand in someone else's shoes' and feel what they feel is an impossibility. What we call empathy is not a magical or telepathic connection, but an act of imagination borne out of our similarities as human beings. Our ability to do this and to resonate with another person's experience is related to how well we have understood the lessons of life and how able we are to comprehend the other's experience. What is crucial for therapy and for life is not just our similarities but also our differences, our ability to see things from different viewpoints, to entertain alternative meanings. It is to be the same but also different.

Engagement is to let the world and our own actions in it matter to us and to let ourselves care about our life and actively connect with it. We can either try to detach ourselves as much as possible and become withdrawn from our experience in order not to feel the hurt and difficulties that living involves. Or we can be fully engaged and passionately live our lives to the full no matter what.

Faith is at the root of every meaningful action. We need to have a personal value system that guides our actions and meanings. The paradox of faith is that we can never be certain of anything but we have to act as if it is so, in full knowledge that it may not be. This produces anxiety which we try to reduce by seeking certainty. Kierkegaard spoke of taking a leap of faith and living like a knight of faith, which means to live in a way that is fully engaged and where we do not try to exempt ourselves from life by denial or special pleading.

Freedom is prominent in all existential thinking. While we have a desire for a firm and permanent moral code we know that one does not exist, and we are therefore free to make our own and to be responsible for living up to it. As Sartre says, 'We are condemned to be free', meaning that making something of our lives within the constraints we all have is no one's responsibility but our own. This also means that we have to be prepared to think about an issue anew each time it presents itself to us. To be free is not an option, but a given: human beings are fundamentally free and capable of many different modes of being.

Givens. These are the conditions of existence, each of which has an unsolvable dilemma at its core. Also known as Ultimate Concerns, they each relate to one of the four worlds: the physical, the social, the psychological and the spiritual. Some of the inevitable givens of the human condition are that we are born to die, that we are always with others and that we have to make our own decisions to the best of our abilities. We have to work for our living and we will inevitably falter and fail, we shall also be in doubt and feel guilt, know hardship, illness, doubt and despair. At the same time it is a given that we have the capacity for consciousness which allows us to rise above all of these givens.

Guilt in an existential sense refers not simply to having done something wrong in a legal or common law way. It refers to a sense of a debt or unease because of having evaded or denied the givens of our existence or having betrayed our moral or relational obligations to ourselves or others as fellow beings. The ultimate arbiter of whether something is 'wrong' or not is not whether the culture deems it so but whether it is coherent with the person's value system which has been developed in the light of the givens of existence.

Intentionality is a fundamental given of the nature of our consciousness: that we are always conscious of something. There can be no human activity, physical, mental, emotional or otherwise without it having a certain direction, intention, object and purpose. Often it is enough to become aware of what our original intentions are if we want to live more in tune with ourselves.

Knowing/Unknowing. Uncertainty/Certainty. Some things, few things, are knowable and these are likely to be physical, factual and everyday. When enquiring into existence and meaning, however, we need to suspend, but not negate, what we think we know. We temporarily become unknowing, which means that we are open to surprise, to discovery, to something we did not expect. We are once again naïve as children and full of wonder for what is. This is often experienced as doubt or self-doubt, for in this process everything is in question. This leads inevitably to the anxiety of uncertainty which we may try to remove by prematurely coming to certainty – persuading ourselves that we know, when we do not. This is where faith and the leap of faith are important.

Leaping in/leaping ahead. Terms used by Heidegger. Leaping in (or jumping in) refers to when, usually out of their personal anxiety, a person takes over and suggests, directs or advises the other in such a manner that another person's autonomy is disabled. Leaping ahead (or jumping ahead), by contrast, refers to an attitude of care for the other which acknowledges and respects their autonomy. In leaping ahead we are available and prepared for the other's discovery of the road ahead with all its obstacles and opportunities, without forcing their hand or making them decide which way to turn at the crossroads.

Meaning and purpose/Meaninglessness. The desire and need for a personally defined meaning and purpose to life is central to existential therapy as is the belief that a person is able to define it for themselves. The ability to define meaning and purpose can only be resiliently arrived at when the person is able to confront the possibility of meaninglessness.

Ontological/Ontic. A distinction made by Heidegger and other philosophers to refer to the difference and relationship between, on the one hand, the essential, necessary and universally valid conditions of human existence – the ontological – and, on the other hand, and the concrete, changing and practical aspects of existence – the ontic. Existential therapists endeavour to bring clients back to the root of their everyday (ontic) problems so they can be seen in the light of the inevitable (ontological) givens of existence. For example, ontological anxiety arising from the inevitability of death and ageing may lead one person to ontically attempt to deny ageing and hence death by cosmetic surgery, another to desire immortality through fame and a third to want to commit suicide so as to escape from the perceived threat.

Paradox. Human existence is paradoxical in that, for example, we can only come truly to life by facing up to the reality of imminent death. Paradoxes are part of life and the existential therapist does not aim to eliminate them but to live constructively with their tension. Indeed, it is this tension that creates the force of life.

Possibility. This does not refer just to what might happen in an everyday sense but to the essential freedom of humankind to choose our actions and live with the consequences. It is often referred to as potentiality. Heidegger claimed that potentiality was always greater than actuality.

Relationship. Existential thinking rejects the notion of the individual person who has relationships with others and with the world, for the idea that person is no more and no less than their relationships. Human beings are essentially relational. We cannot be without a world, without others and without consciousness which is essentially relational in nature. This goes deeper than simply needing relationships in a social sense. The person does not exist separately from their relationships. As with the body, a person does not have relationships, they are their relationships. With respect to therapy, the nature and quality of the relationship determine how well the therapy progresses. It is the ways in which the therapist and client strive to have a true dialogue and together overcome the obstacles they face, that constitute the work of therapy.

Self. Existential authors reject the idea of the self as something which is fixed in favour of the self as a process. It makes more sense to change the noun 'the self' into a verb 'to selve'. The self is always in flux, always in process of becoming and always in relation. In this sense the statement 'I am an angry sort of person' says, for example, more about the way the speaker restricts their possibility than it says about their 'true' nature.

Thrownness. We are born into this world with no say about where or when or even if we come to life. Our first task therefore is to acknowledge this, to choose it in the sense of owning it. Our life starts from a position of randomness and chance. We have to make something of it by taking opportunities as they pass and in creating something new out of what is given to us.

Time and temporality. Time is one of the boundaries to human existence – the way we live our lives is defined by how we see death and the passing of all things, including ourselves. Temporality is the quality of living in time. We do not have or use or waste time, we *are* time. Time is manifest in us, for time is transformation and human beings are the instruments and the place of change.

Truth is usually defined as what is factually correct or real. Existential thinkers are concerned with truth as a value. This is not just a subjective evaluation – 'It feels right so it must be true', but an evaluation in accordance with the givens, dilemmas and paradoxes of existence. To arrive at truth requires a dialectical combination of subjective, objective and existential factors. It is to be expected that we can rarely know the entire and total truth of anything, but this does not mean that such truth does not exist or that we should not strive for it.

Understanding is an essential value in existential therapy and can be contrasted with the idea of knowledge. Understanding is about an embodied, engaged awareness of something in a meaningful way, rather than in terms of purely being able to quote the facts and figures of something. It is about comprehension rather than about explanation.

Values and beliefs are central to meaning. Psychotherapy is not amoral, not value-free and encouraging a client to examine their values and beliefs in order that they better understand their implications will enable a client to more clearly establish and therefore choose which values to live by and which possibilities to actualize.

Worldview refers to the sense we make of the world we are a part of. There is a paradox in that it provides us with structure, without which we might despair. This explains why we get so attached to our viewpoint. But it also prevents us from considering alternatives and to continue our search for truth.

BIBLIOGRAPHY

BASIC AND INTRODUCTORY TEXTS

Cohn, H. (1997) *Existential Thought and Therapeutic Practice*. London: Sage.
Cooper, M. (2003) *Existential Therapies*. London: Sage.
Cox, G. (2008) *The Sartre Dictionary*. London: Continuum.
Cox, G. (2010) *How to Be an Existentialist: or How to Get Real, Get a Grip and Stop Making Excuses*. London: Continuum.
Danto, A.C. (1991) *Sartre*. London: Fontana.
Deurzen, E. van (1998) *Paradox and Passion in Psychotherapy*. Chichester: Wiley.
Deurzen, E. van (2002) *Existential Counselling and Psychotherapy in Practice*. London: Sage.
Deurzen, E. van (2010) *Everyday Mysteries: Existential Dimensions of Psychotherapy, second edition*. London: Routledge.
Deurzen, E. van and Arnold-Baker C. (eds) (2005) *Existential Perspectives on Human Issues: A Handbook for Therapeutic Practice*. Basingstoke: Palgrave Macmillan.
Deurzen. E. van and Kenward, R. (2005) *Dictionary of Existential Psychotherapy and Counselling*. London: Sage.
Frankl, V.E. (1964) *Man's Search for Meaning*. London: Hodder & Stoughton.
Fromm, E. (1995) *The Art of Loving*. London: HarperCollins.
Laing, R.D. (1960) *The Divided Self*. London: Penguin.
Macquarrie, J. (1972) *Existentialism*. London: Penguin.
May, R. (1977) *The Meaning of Anxiety*. New York: Norton.
May, R. (1969) *Love and Will*. London: Norton.
Spinelli, E. (2005) *The Interpreted World. An Introduction to Phenomenological Psychology*, 2nd edn. London: Sage.
Warnock, M. (1970) *Existentialism*. Oxford: Oxford University Press.
Yalom, I. (1980) *Existential Psychotherapy*. New York: Basic Books.
Yalom, I. (1989) *Love's Executioner and Other Tales of Psychotherapy*. London: Penguin.

FURTHER READING

Adams, M. (2006) 'Towards an existential phenomenological model of life span human development', *Existential Analysis*, 17.2. SEA, pp. 261–280.
Barnett, L. (ed.) (2009) *When Death Enters the Therapeutic Space: Existential Perspectives in Psychotherapy and Counselling*. London: Routledge.

Beauvoir, S. de (1963) *Memoirs of a Dutiful Daughter.* London: Penguin.

Becker E. (1997) *The Denial of Death.* New York: Simon and Schuster.

Binswanger, L. (1963) *Being-in-the-world* (trans. J. Needleman). New York: Basic Books.

Blackman, H.J. (1959) *Six Existentialist Thinkers.* New York: Harper and Row.

Boss, M. (1957) *The Analysis of Dreams.* London: Rider.

Boss, M. (1963) *Psychoanalysis and Daseinsanalysis.* New York: Basic Books.

Buber, M. (1958) *I and Thou* (trans. G. Smith). Edinburgh: T&T Clark (original work published 1923).

Burston, D. (1998) 'Heideggers influence on R.D.Laing', *Existential Analysis*, 9.2 SEA, pp. 58–71.

Camus, A. (2005) *The Myth of Sisyphus* (trans. J. O'Brien). London: Penguin (original work published 1942).

Cohn, H. (2002) *Heidegger and the Roots of Existential Therapy.* London: Continuum.

Collins, J. (2000) *Heidegger and the Nazis.* London: Icon.

Cox, G. (2009) *Sartre and Fiction.* London: Continuum.

Deurzen, E. van (2008) *Psychotherapy and the Quest for Happiness.* London: Sage.

Deurzen, E. van and Young S. (2009) *Existential Perspectives on Supervision.* Basingstoke: Palgrave Macmillan.

Friedman, M. (ed.) (1991) *The Worlds of Existentialism.* London: Humanities.

Fromm, E. (1995) *The Art of Loving.* London: Thorsons.

Fry, E. (1966) *Cubism.* London: Thames and Hudson.

Graves, R. (1992) *The Greek Myths.* London: Penguin.

Guignon, C. (2004) *On Being Authentic.* Abingdon: Routledge.

Heidegger, M. (1962) *Being and Time* (trans. J. Macquarrie and E.S. Robinson). New York: Harper and Row (original work published 1962).

Jacobsen, B. (2007) *Invitation to Existential Psychology.* Chichester: Wiley.

Kemp, R. (2009) 'The lived-body of drug addiction', *Existential Analysis*, 20.1 SEA, pp. 120–133.

Kierkegaard, S. (1970) *The Concept of Dread* (trans. W. Lowrie). Princeton, NJ: Princeton University Press (original work published 1844).

Laing, R.D. (1961) *Self and Others.* Harmondsworth: Penguin.

Laing, R.D. (1967) *The Politics of Experience.* Harmondsworth: Penguin.

Langdridge, D. (2005). 'The child's relations with others' – Merleau-Ponty, embodiment and psychotherapy, *Existential Analysis*, 16.1, SEA, pp. 87–100.

Langdridge, D. (2007) *Phenomenological Psychology: Theory, Research and Method.* Harlow: Pearson Education.

Macann, C. (1993) *Four Phenomenological Philosophers.* London: Routledge.

Madison G. (2004) 'Hospital philosophy: an existential-phenomenological perspective'. In M.Luca (ed), *The Therapeutic Frame in the Clinical Context: Integrative Perspectives.* London: Routledge.

May, R. (1983) *The Discovery of Being.* New York: Norton.

May, R., Angel, E. and Ellenberger, H.F. (1958) *Existence.* New York: Basic Books.

Mearns, D. and Cooper, M. (2005) *Working at Relational Depth in Counselling and Psychotherapy.* London: Sage.

Merleau-Ponty, M. (1962) *The Phenomenology of Perception* (trans. C. Smith). London: Routledge (original work published 1945).

Milton M. and Judd D. (1999) 'The dilemma that is assessment', *Existential Analysis*, 10.1, pp. 102–104.

Moran, D. (2000) *Introduction to Phenomenology.* London: Routledge.

Moustakas. C. (1994) *Phenomenological Research Methods.* London: Sage.

Neibuhr, R. (1987) *The Essential Reinhold Neibuhr: Selected Essays and Addresses* (edited by R.M. Brown). Yale: Yale University Press.

Nietzsche, F. (1961) *Thus Spoke Zarathustra* (trans. R.J. Hollingdale). Harmondsworth: Penguin (original work published 1883).

Rowley, H. (2007) *Tête-à-tête: The Lives and Loves of Simone de Beauvoir and Jean-Paul Sartre.* London: Vintage.

Ryle, G. (1949) *The Concept of Mind.* Chicago: University of Chicago Press.

Sartre, J.-P. (1973) *Existentialism and Humanism* (trans. P. Mairet). London: Methuen (original work published 1946).

Sartre, J.-P. (1985) *Sketch for a Theory of the Emotions* (trans. P. Mairet). London: Methuen (original work published 1939).

Sartre, J.-P. (2000) *Words* (trans. I. Clephane). London: Penguin (original work published 1961).

Sartre, J.-P. (2003) *Being and Nothingness: An Essay in Phenomenological Ontology* (trans. H.E. Barnes). London: Routledge (original work published 1943).

Schneider, K. (2007) *Existential-integrative Psychotherapy: Guideposts to the Core of Practice.* London: Routledge.

Spinelli, E. (2009) *Practising Existential Psychotherapy. The Relational World.* London: Sage.

Stolorow, R. (2007) *Trauma and Human Existence.* New York: The Analytic Press.

Strasser, F. (1999) *Emotions: Experiences in Existential Psychotherapy and Life.* London: Duckworth.

Strasser, F. and Strasser, A. (1997) *Existential Time-Limited Therapy.* Chichester: Wiley.

Szasz, T.S. (1984) *The Myth of Mental Illness.* New York: HarperCollins.

Thompson M. Guy. (2002) 'The existential dimension to working through', *Existential Analysis,* 13.1, SEA, p. 46–67.

Tillich, P. (2000) *The Courage to Be.* London: Yale University Press (original work published 1952).

Yalom, I. (2003) *The Gift of Therapy.* London: Piatkus.

NOVELS AND PLAYS

Ballard, J.G. (1997) *Cocaine Nights.* London: Flamingo.

Ballard, J.G. (2006) *Empire of the Sun.* London: Harper.

Boyd, W. (1987) *The New Confessions.* London: Hamish Hamilton.

Boyd, W. (2002) *Any Human Heart.* London: Hamish Hamilton.

Camus, A. (2006) *The Outsider* (trans. J. Laredo). London: Penguin (original work published 1942).

Carroll, L. (2007) *Through the Looking Glass.* London: Penguin (original work published 1871).

de Saint-Exupéry, A. (1991) *The Little Prince* (trans. K. Woods). Harmondsworth: Puffin (original work published 1943).

Dostoyevsky, F. (2003) *Crime and Punishment* (trans. D. McDuff). London: Vintage (original work published 1866).

Fielding, H. (1997) *Bridget Jones Diary.* London: Picador.

Highsmith, P. (1999) *The Talented Mr. Ripley.* London: Vintage.

Hornby, N. (1996) *High Fidelity.* London: Indigo.

Kesey, K. (1973) *One Flew over the Cuckoo's Nest.* London: Picador.

Koestler, A. (1994) *Darkness at Noon* (trans. D. Hardy). London: Penguin (original work published 1940).

Powell, A. (1997) *A Dance to the Music of Time.* London: Arrow (original works published 1951–75).

Pullman, P. (2007) *His Dark Materials.* London: Scolastic.

Rhinehart, L. (1999) *The Dice Man.* London: HarperCollins.

Salinger, J.D. (1994) *A Catcher in the Rye.* London: Penguin (original work published 1951).

Sartre, J.P. (2000) *Huis Clos and Other Plays (The Respectable Prostitute, Lucifer and the Lord)* trans. K. Black. London: Penguin. (Original works published 1945, 1951, 1947.)

Sartre, J.-P. (2000) *Nausea* (trans. R. Baldick). London: Penguin (original work published 1938).

Sartre, J.-P. (2002) *The Roads to Freedom (The Age of Reason, The Reprieve, Iron in the Soul)* (trans. E. Sutton, G. Hopkins). London: Penguin (original works published 1945–49).

Shakespeare, W. *Hamlet.*

Vickers, S. (2006) *The Other Side of You.* London: Fourth Estate.

Watterson, B. (1995) *Calvin and Hobbes.* Kansas City, MO: Universal Press Syndicate.

Wilder, T. (2000) *The Bridge of San Luis Rey.* London: Penguin.

Yalom, I. (1992) *When Nietzsche Wept.* London: Harper.

FILMS

Woody Allen (1989) *Crimes and Misdemeanours.* USA: Orion Pictures.

Michelangelo Antonioni (1975) *The Passenger.* Italy: Compagnia Cinematografica Champion.

Ingmar Bergman (1957) *The Seventh Seal.* Sweden: Svensk Filmindustri.

Claude Berri (1986) *Jean de Florette* and *Manon des Sources.* France: DD Productions.

Luc Besson (1997) *The Fifth Element.* France: Gaumont.

Frank Capra (1946) *It's a Wonderful Life.* USA: Liberty Films.

Steven Daldry (2002) *The Hours.* USA/UK: Paramount.

Mel Gibson (1995) *Braveheart.* USA/Icon Entertainment.

Peter Jackson (2001/2/3) *The Lord of the Rings* Trilogy. New Zealand/USA: New Line Cinema.

Akira Kurosawa (1954) *Seven Samurai.* Japan: Toho Company.

Roman Polanski (2002) *The Pianist.* France/Germany/UK/Poland: R.P. Productions.

Martin Scorsese (1988) *The Last Temptation of Christ.* USA/Cineplex-Odeon Films.

Steven Soderbergh (2002) *Solaris.* USA: Twentieth Century Fox.

Wim Wenders (1987) *Wings of Desire.* West Germany/France: Road Movies Filmproduktion.

INDEX

Note: page numbers in *italic* refer to the glossary.

absurdity 20
activity/active living 73, 89
addiction 91, 101, 107, 111, 115
agoraphobia 57
Alcoholics Anonymous 21
Allen, Woody 17, 99
aloneness 18
anger 84
anxiety 150
    authenticity/inauthenticity 90–6
    existential concept of 24
    tension and conflicts examined 58–60
    therapist's 47
assessment and diagnosis 124–6
assumptions 56, 148, *150*
    of existential therapy 41–2
    mistaken 45–6
    questioning of 41–2
    relationship to givens 42
    therapist's own 43–4, 46
attending and describing 42–3
attention 24, 31, 36, 42–6, 51, 60
authenticity 90–2, *150*
    existential cycle of 93
    detecting presence/absence of 92–6
authority, therapist's 94, 110
autonomy *see* freedom and autonomy
awareness 44

bad faith/mauvaise foi 15, 90, 92, *150*
being-in-the-world 21
beliefs *see* values and beliefs
bias, therapist's 46
Bingswanger 1, 14
blame 89, 119, 138
blind spots 44
body, the 24–6
Body Dysmorphic Disorder 25
Boss, Medard 2, 14
boundaries 60–3, 127

bracketing 43, 46, 55, 56, 147
Buber, Martin 14, 21, 110

Calvin and Hobbes 91
Camus, Albert 15
Cannon, Betty 2
CBT 2
care, duty of 61
certainty *153*
change *151*
choice 10, 15, 19, 59, 73–4, 80–1, 110, 148–9, *151*
    and responsibility 89–90
claustrophobia 57
client
    learning new skills *see* learning process
    suitability to therapy 41
    therapeutic needs and wishes 101–2
client–therapist relationship *see* therapeutic
    relationship
closed questions 48
cogito 43
coherence (of interpretation) 53
commitment 12, 19, 23, 114, 118, 122, *151*
compass of emotions 80–5
competitiveness 110–12
complacency 142
conflicts and tensions 18, 102–4
connectivity (of interpretation) 53
contracts 130–1
control 109–10
Cooper, Mick, 2
Copernicus, 20
Crimes and Midemeanors 89
crisis 118–19, 151

Darwin 20
de Beauvoir, Simone 15
death *see* life and death
decisions *see* choice
denial and evasion 92

descriptive analysis 47–8, *151*
  opening out a dialogue 50
determinism *151*
diagnosis 125
dialectics 23, *151*
dialogue 63–4, 145, *152*
dilemmas *see* paradoxes and dilemmas
dimensions of existence 16–21
  four worlds framework 146–7
directiveness 69–70
dominance 18
door-handle comments 133
dreams 96–100

Eigentlichkeit 91
Eigenwelt 19
Einstein 20
embodiment *152*
emotions 80–1, 147
  assumptions and mistaken
      feelings 45–6
  common feelings in therapy 138
  confusing complexity of 83–5
  emotional compass 81–5
  and phenomenological questioning 85–6
  thinking and feeling 84–5
  traced back to dilemmas 87–9
empathy 31, 104, *152*
ending
  individual sessions 132–4
  therapy 135–7, 139
engagement *152*
envy 82, 83
Epoché 43, 50
equalization 48–9
  breaking the principle of 51
essence 9–10
ethics 63, 66
  personal code of 76–7
evaluation 148
evasion and denial 92
existence
  dimensions of 16–21
  and essence 9–10
  philosophical questions about
      7–8, 11–12
existential therapy, overview of
  basic assumptions 41
  description of 7–11
  development and tradition 2–3
  general aims 4, 11–13
  major contributing philosophers 13–15
  principle concepts 15–26
  skills 3–4
  summary of principles and practice 144–9
expectations 149

experience, openness to 57–60
explanation *151*
explicit, the 145
expression 72–3

faith 118–19, *152*
fears 82, 147, 149
  and freedoms 58–60, 74
feelings *see* emotions
fees 79, 131–2
four worlds framework 146–7
  see also dimensions
frame 62, 76, 126–8
Frankl, Victor 2
freedom and autonomy *150, 152–3*
  freedoms and fears 58–60, 74
  respect for client's autonomy 69–70
  and responsibility 19, 92–3
Frued, S. 1, 7, 14
Fromm, Erich 130
future, reference to 93

Galileo 20
givens (of existence) 15, *153*
  and anxiety 24
  assumptions related to 42
  choice as 89
  life's reminders of 90–100
Greek philosophy 8, 11–12
guilt 36, 81, 83, 90, 92, 138, *153*
  and inauthenticity 92–3

Heidegger, Martin 2, 9, 21, 24, 32, 69,
      91, *152, 153, 154*
  biography 14
Heisenberg 20
hermeneutic 43, 54
homework 130, 132
hope 21, 82, 83
horizontalization 50–1
human existence *see* existence
Husserl, Edmund 14, 40, 43
  biography 13–14

ideals 149
imagination 96
implicit, the 146
inauthenticity *see* authenticity
individuality 18
intentionality, principle of 40, 43, *153*
interdependence 108
interpretive intervention 52–5
  opening out dialogue 54–5, 55–6
introspection 39–40
intuitions 84
issues, identifying 73–4, 146

Jaspers, Karl 14
jealousy 82
joy 82, 83
jumping in/jumping ahead 69, *153–4*

Kierkegaard, Søren 13
knowing *153*

language, use of 48, 147
    expressing emotions 86–9
    pronoun switching 93, 94–5
    second language 86–7
    and values 78
leaping in/leaping ahead 69, *153–4*
learning process, therapy as 137
    clarification 137–8
    difficulties and giving up 138–40
    finding new ways 140–1
    gaining competence/complacency 141–3
life and death *151*
    addressing the paradox/dilemma of 105–7
    and close relationships 113
    living in time 22, *155*
    the physical dimension 17–18
listening skills 60
logotheraphy 2
love 82, 83
Love and Will 130

map 16, 40, 103
Marcel, Gabriel 14
May, Rollo 14, 130
meaning *154*
    and verification 144, 147–8
meaninglessness 20, *154*
Mearns, Dave 2
medication 102
Merleau-Ponty, Maurice 15
mind–body relationship 24–6
Mitwelt 18, 107
money 62, 78, 131
monologue 63–4
mortality *see* life and death
mutuality 63

Nietzsche, Friedrich 21, 25, 133
    biography 13
Noema and Noesis 43
note-taking 126

ontic 101, 154
ontological 24, 58, 91, 101, 118, *154*
openness 57–60, 148
options *see* choice
original project/choice 80, 113–14, 116, 147

paradoxes and dilemmas *152, 154*
    client's views and responses 102–4
    emotions and dilemmas 87–9
    living with 23, 55, 90–1, 95, 148

paradoxes and dilemmas *cont.*
    personal dimension 115
    physical dimension 105–7, 113
    social dimension 108–9
    spiritual dimension 119–20
passivity/passive living 72, 89
past, the
    client references to 95
    giving meaning to 114
Pavlov 7
Perls 7
persecutor role 110–11
personal dimension, the 16, 19, 146
    the original project 113–14
    paradox and dilemma 115
    themes and issues 73–4
    therapeutic approaches to 115–17
personal style, developing 149
phenomenology 39–40, 145
    in everyday life 57
    the practice of 42–3
    questioning and emotions 85–6
philosophers 12, 13–15
philosophical basis of therapy
        7–9, 11–12, 144–5
physical dimension, the 16, 17–18, 146
    paradox and dilemma of 105–6
    themes and issues 73–4
    therapeutic approaches to 105–7
Plato 12
Picasso 6
possibility *154*
practice principles, summary of 145–9
preconceptions *see* assumptions
pride 82
projects 113–14, 147, 149
prompts 145
    see also questions and questioning
pronoun switching 93, 94–5
purpose 154
    and absurdity 21

questions and questioning 41
    and descriptive analysis 47–8
    philosophical/meaning of life 7–8
    prompts 145
    questioning assumptions 40–2
    self-directed questions 44–5, 46
    and statements of verification 52

rapport 48
reactivity 94
reflection 10–11, 73
relationships 154
    client–therapist *see* therapeutic relationship
    conflict of values 78
    layers of 107–8
    roles played 110–11
    and the social dimension 18
    therapeutic approaches to 108–13

relevance (of interpretation) 54
religion 20, 21, 118, 122
reluctance 134
rescuer role 110–11
resistance 134
responsibility, personal 11, 19, 151
   and choice 89–90
Rogers 7
Ryle, Gilbert 25

Sartre, Jean-Paul 9, 19, 21, 30, 32, 92, 110, 114, *151, 152*
   biography 15
Schneider, Kirk 2
sedimentation 57
self, sense of 10, 57, 72, 114, 154
self-blame 119
self-deception 92, 96, 146
self-disclosure 65–8
self-expression 72–3
selve, to 71
sensations 85
sessions, management of 61–2
   beginning and ending sessions 132–4
   contracts 130–1
   fees 131–2
   first session 128–30
   location and setting 127–8
   missed sessions 79, 134
   note-taking 126
   preparations and attention 44–5, 125
   termination of therapy 135–7
   working through/reluctance and resistance 133–4
Shakespeare, *Hamlet*, 89
shame 82–3
silence, openness to 60
simplicity (of interpretation) 53
social dimension, the 16, 18, 146
   paradox and dilemma 108–9
   relationship difficulties 107–13
   themes and issues 73–4
social isolation 113
Socratic method 12
sorrow 82
Spinelli, Ernesto 2
spiritual dimension, the 16, 20–1, 147
   paradox and dilemma 119–20
   religion 21–2
   themes and issues 74
   therapeutic approaches to 117–22
storytelling 123–4
structural analysis, of client's existence 148–9
supervision 44, 45, 139
symptom relief 101–2

temporality 22, *155*
tensions 147
tensions *see* conflicts and tensions
termination *see* ending

terminology 8, *150–5*
territory *see* map
The Art of Loving 130
The Roads to freedom 110
themes
   identifying 73–4, 146
   working with 74–6
theoretical framework *see* existential therapy
therapeutic change *see* learning process
therapeutic relationship 48, 70, 113
   and assessment 125
   boundaries 60–3, 127
   care and consistency 61–2
   collaboration 145, 148
   difficulties ending therapy 136–7
   mutuality 63
   and self-disclosure 65–8
   settings and frame 126–8
   significance of door-handle comments 133
   trust and control 63, 109–10
   and value systems 79
therapies compared 1–2, 8–9
thrownness 15, *155*
Tillich, Paul 21
   biography 14
time 22, *155*
trauma 118–19
trust 63, 109–10
truth 146, 155

Überwelt 20
ultimate rescuer 106
Umwelt 17, 105
uncertainty *153*
understanding *155*
unknowing 52, *153*

values and beliefs *155*
   double-sided and dilemmas 87–9
   identifying 76–7, 148
   and the spiritual dimension 20, 119, 146
   therapist's own 79–80
   working with client's 77–9
verification
   defined 43
   and interpretation 50–5, 148
victim role 110–11, 114
vocabulary *see* language

wisdom 11, 29, 34, 75, 103, 122
working through 133–4
worldview 20, 147, *155*
   complexities and subtleties 147
   and interpretation 52–3
   and mind–body relationships 24–6
   significance of themes 74
   wider perspective 55

Supporting researchers for more than forty years

Research methods have always been at the core of SAGE's publishing. Sara Miller McCune founded SAGE in 1965 and soon after she published SAGE's first methods book, *Public Policy Evaluation*. A few years later, she launched the Quantitative Applications in the Social Sciences series – affectionately known as the 'little green books'.

Always at the forefront of developing and supporting new approaches in methods, SAGE published early groundbreaking texts and journals in the fields of qualitative methods and evaluation.

Today, more than forty years and two million little green books later, SAGE continues to push the boundaries with a growing list of more than 1,200 research methods books, journals, and reference works across the social, behavioural, and health sciences.

From qualitative, quantitative and mixed methods to evaluation, SAGE is the essential resource for academics and practitioners looking for the latest in methods by leading scholars.

www.sagepublications.com